MW00426504

SHADOW SHAPES

A WOUNDED JOURNALIST IN WWI FRANCE

October 1918—*May* 1919

BY

ELIZABETH SHEPLEY SERGEANT

"I was wounded in the house of my friends"

1920

Contents

PUBLISHER'S NOTES

In this work, for which American journalist and writer Elizabeth Sergeant is best remembered, she gives us a view of the end of World War I through the eyes of one trained to see dispassionately. Severely wounded, at times frightened, surrounded by pain and suffering, Sergeant nevertheless delivers an amazing analysis of war and what it does to soldier and civilian alike.

Elizabeth "Elsie" Shepley Sergeant was born April 23, 1881, in Winchester, Massachusetts to Charles Spencer Sergeant, a Boston merchant, and Elizabeth "Bessie" Blake Shepley. Elsie was the eldest of three daughters. She graduated from Bryn Mawr and immediately captured the attention of writer Willa Cather, who published Sergeant's article on sweatshops in *McClure's*.

Elsie never married but in 1929 her sister, Katharine, married a young E.B. White, co-author of the famous book *The Elements of Style*, commonly referred to as Strunk and White. Katherine graduated in the Bryn Mawr College class of 1914. She began working for Harold Ross at *The New Yorker* in 1925, six months after its inception.

Sergeant traveled extensively during her life for her writing career, before and after the war. On September 4, 1917, she sailed on the SS *Rochambeau* for France. On her August passport application she noted the object of her visit as "To study problems of reconstruction as a correspondent and representative of *The New Republic* [magazine]." The application indicated that she intended to return within six months. In 1918, she returned to France again, only to end up in a long hospital stay after being wounded by an explosion.

Her vibrant writing from the Western front was the kind of journalism that humanizes and sees between the flashes and thunder for something less obvious. It was not political writing. Here she is from *The New Republic*:

Paris Under Fire

"MARCH 9th: Last night we had our second big air raid. As soon as the sharp sound of the explosions had died away—before the French cannonading had stopped and well before the berloque announced the end—I stuck my head out of my window. Utter blackness, blackness impenetrable, blackness that denied the very possibility of light, yet through it, on the street below, was already traveling something warm and vibrant and human: the Paris crowd. It was as if a river, obstructed for a moment, had found its normal course again."

For a time after her return from France, she recuperated at the home of her widowed father in Rockland County, New York, where one of her sisters also lived (1925 New York state census). Eventually she was advised by her doctor to move to New Mexico.

Into the mid-1930s she lived in Taos and wrote about New Mexico and the Pueblo Indians. She even wrote the Commissioner of Indian Affairs about observations of problems on the reservations.

At 79 she published a well-received biography of Robert Frost in 1960, upon which she had spent ten years in the making. Frost, an intensely private man, had given his assent to the biography in the 1940s. Sergeant rented a house near Frost and spent time with him and his family. She was not a trained biographer and considered herself an intuitive writer. But she eschewed Freudian approaches to biography ("...too theoretical...") and labeled herself a Jungian. All the time she continued to write for various magazines. She also spent time writing at The MacDowell Colony, Peterborough, New Hampshire.

Elizabeth Sergeant died suddenly in New York City on January 26, 1965. Her papers are held at Bryn Mawr and Yale University.

NOTE

I was wounded in the house of my friends

A FEW pages of *Shadow-Shapes*—images and memories of war-time Paris—were first published as correspondence in *The New Republic* during the years 1917-18. But the author owes the whole background of her French war experience to the paper and its Editors, and for their unfailing generosity here makes grateful acknowledgment.

PREFACE

THIS book belongs to the nurses, the doctors, the friends who gathered about my hospital bed in France. Their beautiful kindness was as healing as their care, and I shall never be able to thank them for the part they gave me in the chimerical days which I saw reflected with such vividness in their faces.

The best of what they shared and what they were I have not even tried to set down. But where their faces and their voices seemed symbolic of certain human types and mysteries pondered by all Americans in France in the period between war and peace, I have ventured to quote them and picture them. My wish has been not to change what I saw and heard by a line or a feature, lest the least alteration should do violence to a vast, embracing, unseizable truth that was essentially our common possession. The heightened glow cast by danger and death on the faces of the young, and its fading into the rather flat daylight of survival; the psychological dislocation of the Armistice; the weariness of reconstruction; the shift in Franco-American relations that followed President Wilson's intervention in European affairs; the place of American women in the adventures of the A.E.F.—all this and much more I groped through my illness to understand, as my visitors came and went, and noted on paper and in memory. The journal which has resulted does not pretend to offer more than a marginal commentary. For nobody knows better than an accidentally wounded writer that the real story can only be told by a soldier—perhaps by one of those limping privates whose shadows were always creeping across the Neuilly windows to remind me that in the damp tents where they were continuing the Argonne and the Marne, not in my comfortable gray room, was the substance of America in France.

E. S. S.

August 1920

THE WING OF DEATH

Mont-Notre-Dame October 20, 1918

THEY have stretched a sheet around my cot this morning. It does not shut out the pervasive *poilu* smell. And I can still see the young French soldier directly across the ward. Day and night he lies high against a back-rest. He has a great hole in his abdomen, and a torturing thirst, and cries faintly every two or three minutes:

"Infirmier, infirmier, a boire, a boire."

October 21

THE *poilu* can't be more than twenty. His eyes are caverns, dark wells of pain in a face blanched and shrunk to the angles of the bones beneath. They gaze out from under a shock of lank black hair that seems to grow every hour longer; gaze with the persistently hurt, surprised expression of a child who has put his hand in the fire, and finds that fire burns. When they first began to haunt me, emerging from the murk of the tent and vanishing again, early yesterday morning, I thought they were a sort of symbol. Ether bedazed me and I could not quite grasp the meaning of the symbol. I confused the *poilu* with a black-haired Oklahoma boy whom I found last June in a French hospital at Meaux; alone but for one muttering Arab in a vast, dirty ward; bedbugs crawling over him; blood soaking his shirt and blankets. The most lost and miserable American of all.

Now his face stared at me, gaunt and craggy, from the French soldier's bed. I begged Mercier, my orderly, to change the Oklahoman's blankets; told him that my fellow-countryman could not make his needs understood; insisted eloquently—and heard Mercier laugh—that he should take the "houses" off my legs. I was unable to help so long as their weight pressed me down. Mercier explained that they were not to be removed. But it was the *poilu's* head, glooming clearer and clearer like a tormented ascetic head in a Spanish painting, that at last brought me to myself. I remembered exactly what had happened to me and it seemed—seems now—altogether negligible in the light of that suffering stare.

"Infirmier, à boire—just one little drop?"

Valentin, the cross old orderly who passed just then, tells him brutally to shut his mouth. It will be wet in due time, not before. And Valentin shuffles on, in his felt slippers, and his streaked grey-blue clothes, which depend flabbily from a loosely hinged backbone. Here comes Mercier, taking temperatures. Mercier is a generation younger than Valentin. He swings his muscular hips as he walks, as if he belonged to the Breton sea. But it seems that *dans le civil* he is a *coiffeur* at Le Mans. Mercier declares, after consulting his wrist-watch, that *le petit* must wait exactly nineteen minutes for the next swallow of champagne.

Miss Bullard, meanwhile, briskly reminds Mercier—who continues to stand poised, twisting waxed blond moustaches—that it is nearly ten; only half the temperatures taken; no dressings done; several stimulations to be given men who are very low; the surgeons due on rounds at any moment. Mercier looks crestfallen. Murmurs, with a half glance in my direction:

"Je n'ai pas l' esprit au travail ce matin—my mind isn't on my work this morning."

Miss Bullard, as she hurries on, gives the little soldier a smile from under her white veil that brings a momentary look of peace into his bewildered eyes. But soon the monotonous whimper begins again:

"A drink, a drink"—he is wanly beseeching me now, as if I ought to be able to rise on my two splints and slip him a few drops from the bottle on the shelf over his bed. A woman—not nursing—in an evacuation hospital—during an attack....

Have I said anything else to myself these two endless days and nights? Raw flesh—shattered bones—pain—fever—thirst—disability—death. Why should I be caught up into this revelation of the ultimate of war unless I can turn my understanding to some service?

There is one unbearable sound. A dull, pierced, animal plaint, nothing like the usual moan of pain, or the cries of the wounded who are being dressed. A sort of sigh went up from the whole ward when it began. Miss Bullard dropped everything and ran, though the man she left is only a little less in need. Her look is fixed as she prepares her hypodermic in the alcove beyond my bed.

She works so swiftly, so gallantly. Did she realize when she put me in this corner near her table of supplies, the satisfaction I should get from the perfection of her technique? From simply *seeing* her, single-handed, single-hearted, direct a whole hospital and meet the outstanding needs of her twenty-four *grands blesses?* She must have known it would be a spiritual substitute for the nursing she would be giving me under other circumstances. She can do only the essential now. Racked and lacerated as I feel, I am yet one of the least serious cases. Two thirds of the patients are just barely being kept alive. She literally does not stop one second in the twelve hours she is here. Even so, she is consumed (as I have seen Lucinda consumed at Dr. Blake's hospital this last six months) by the desperate need to do more. Miss Bullard sleeps a mile away, in a ruined village, in a room with no window-glass and no stove. She has to walk there again for lunch. Only a sort of exaltation keeps the human machine going through such stress. She must have been drawing for months on springs far deeper than the normal springs of human energy and endurance.

She sends Mercier to tell me, as her fingers fit rubber tubes together, that she will make me comfortable for the day before long. I am ashamed that I do want to have my face washed, that I do want to feel her soothing touch at my feet. The soldier she had to desert is two beds away from me. His face was considerably shot to pieces. He has to be fed through a tube. But he lies there dumbly patient and quiescent.

Afternoon

YES, only those who cannot help themselves ask for anything here at least by day. I believe I was conscious of it even those first irresponsible hours. For when I heard my own voice calling Mercier—as it did so often—I was amazed and repentant. Extraordinary how quickly one becomes part of the mechanism; how one can bear anything in company. Just because it is war, and must be borne. *C'est la fatalite*. Inevitable. Irrevocable. Immutable.

Interminable. Nothing exists, or ever will exist but this khaki tent pitched in the mud; this rain that drips, drips through the roof; these two blind rows of closed window-squares; this stove that smokes; this backbreaking cot; these grimed and stuffy blankets; this clinging smell of damp, and coal-smoke, and iodine, and disinfectant, and suppurating wounds, and human sweat and dirt. Yet to name the obvious discomforts is to exaggerate them. They become submerged in a more profound initiation—an initiation which is almost a compensation.

A visitor has made this clear to me. The *medecin-chef,* full of apologies for not having himself visited me sooner, ushered him in. They came mincing down the ward together, between desperately sick men of whom they seemed quite unaware; the *medecin-chef,* in his unsullied horizon blue, looking a sort of operatic tenor after the hard-pressed, shabby surgeons I have so far seen; the visitor an elongated, dapper personage from the Maison de la Presse. He had journeyed all the way from Paris, in his best rue Francois I' uniform, to bring me "the condolences of the French Government."

A camp-stool was provided. The stove was belching saffron clouds that rose and hung under the floppy canvas. The attention of the *blesses* was glumly superior. The visitor sat there shivering, coughing, fondling an imperceptible moustache with one nervous hand, blinking away smoky tears, as he made polite conversation. Drops trickled down his neck. His reddened eyes took in my bandages, the "cradle" that raised the bedclothes over my feet. But what they dwelt on with fascinated commiseration were the fragment of my skirt that Miss Bullard had pinned about my shoulders and the pillow she had improvised,—Gertrude's coon-coat, which luckily came through intact. (The hospital has no bed-pillows, and only three back-rests.)

"How uncomfortable you must be, Mademoiselle!"

Poor Monsieur, not nearly so uncomfortable as you, though I tried hard to make your half-hour as easy as I could.

One thing I do mind—greasy old tin plates. I can swallow sickish tea, and *limonade* that never saw a lemon, and gratefully, when

Mercier holds the china " duck " to my lips. But when he brings me onion-scented soup, full of vague, floating vegetables, in an ancient, ancient tin receptacle.... He was very proud at lunch-time. He had succeeded in finding an egg, a very round and orange fried egg which skated madly over that dubious black surface. It was perfectly cold. But I choked it down with a humble fear that I was being pampered.

I *am* pampered. I have sheets. Miss Bullard, of course, produced them. And though she had been up all my first night, she went the long distance to her room and brought back a nightgown and comb of her own. Even a new toothbrush, and a box of "Dorin Rose."* (Dorin Rose! The visitor should have noted that pathetic effort to be faithful to feminine tradition.) As my cot is curtained off, she keeps the window in the Bessano tent open over my head. The French surgeons allow no air to blow through the ward, and as soon as she is gone at night the orderly zealously shuts my porthole from the outside.

**A premier perfume.*

I dread the moment when Miss Bullard goes for a good many reasons—the moment when I am left alone in this world of anguished men. It is then that it is most intolerable to be helpless. If only I could do the small things the orderlies neglect once the nurse's eye is off them. Even during Miss Bullard's lunch-hour—if she takes a lunch-hour—there is a more restless spirit among the *blesses*. They talk of her from bed to bed. Her *drôle de francais,* her funny French, which they delight in; her capacity; her sympathy; her well-earned *Croix de Guerre*. After all, they say, why should an American woman be nursing Frenchmen? There are no French nurses here. *"Elle a bien du merile."* But soon they begin to wonder why she isn't back; begin to fuss. And at night, when she has given the last hypodermic, and put on her cape and stolen out, black desolation settles down over the tent.

October 22

LAST night the ward was like a sombre tunnel, full of smoke and noxious gas; monstrous moving shadows; painful reverberation.

Feet, feet, trampling, trampling; *brancardiers* [stretcher bearers], shuffling into the tent with new burdens. Shall I ever forget how their feet are sucked into the glutinous mud of the Marne? It is as if the mud were insatiable. And it gives out, in the dark and silence, the muted sound of all those other stretcher-bearing feet which it has sucked and strained at for four years. Mont-Notre-Dame was an important French hospital centre until the Germans took it last spring. On the recovered ground a French hospital has been planted again. And yet again come the *brancardiers* bearing still, horizontal shapes on their shoulders, shapes once vivid, earth-loving; now writhen, agonized, indifferent. War is a doom, trampling, shuffling itself out to eternity.

And the orderly on duty last night was a doddering old fellow who let the men get completely out of hand. It is no kindness, as I have discovered. The least serious cases make the worst row. The thigh began it:

"Ô la, la, la, la, ô la, la, la, la"—each "ô" a note higher in the scale and the *"la's"* running down in Tetrazzini's manner:

"C'est-il-mal-heureux, c'est-il-mal-heureux," responds the arm in the next bed, who has no intention of being outdone.

"Damnee guerre, damnee guerre," echoes the "shoulder blade."

This had been going on perhaps fifteen minutes when the little *poilu* opposite me tore off his bandages. Patience is a terrible virtue. Would not wars end if ten thousand wounded men tore off their bandages and bled to death? But the process is hideous. The *vieux,* badly scared, called Mercier, and with much stifled gasping and cursing they together bound him up again in the flicker of a lantern.

Can it be that only forty or fifty miles from here people are discussing, over partridge and *fraises des bois,* whether it would be better for Foch to accept an armistice or to push the Germans to a complete *debdcle?* Better give a few months more, and several thousands more men, say some. I wish they could spend a night in my cot. Can it be that in Paris I, too, believed in the end of the war? The very evening before my accident, the evening of the day when the French army entered Lille, I came out of the Castiglione, after dinner, into light. *Light* in Paris at eleven o'clock at night. *Light* after nearly four years of war-darkness! Those great torches, flaring brazenly from the Tuileries terrace, on brazen enemy guns strewn over the place de la Concorde, conveyed, as they were intended to do, a sort of shout of triumph. The enemy had been driven so far, so far, that not the boldest or fleetest of his bombers could any longer threaten the heart of France.

Yet here the fear of air raids is not conjured. I shall not soon forget the whirring pulse that throbbed and burrowed into our tent tunnel in the small hours of last night. Ominous, discomposing. Airplanes, squadron after squadron, passing just overhead. Boche or our own? The complete defencelessness I felt so long as the uncertainty lasted made me aware that what I had hitherto taken for moral courage during raids was purely physical; a pair of good legs and a convenient medieval cellar had sustained me. I know something about the psychology of the bomber, too. Great to drop off your load on a group of tents; to get a direct hit, a tongue of flame. (Lord, it was a hospital!)

After all, I am just as bad as the men at night but for New England pride. My soul also escapes from what Jules Romains would call the *unanimisme* of the ward; from the bonds of a common fate which enjoin a decent patience. I become an impotent, aching creature, full of unpleasant holes, lost in a corner of devastated France infinitely remote from every one I care for. The hospital unit had moved up from Château-Thierry the night before I got here. No telephone connection with Paris yet. So I cannot get cables through to my family in America; or to the N.R. I can't even telegraph my brother-in-law, Ernest,* at Dijon; or Colonel Lambert at the Red Cross; or Rick, who has just lost his brother, on top of losing almost his entire squadron in the Argonne, and is due in Paris on leave. He wired me the night before my accident to cable his mother; and there should be an answer by now—and I of no use.

**This was Katherine Sergeant's first husband, Ernest Angell.*

I ask for tea. The orderly comes running. *("ca change, une femme,"* thinks he. And I—"I can't see his dirty hands in the dark.") But tea is no sedative. I hug my stone jar of hot water tight but I can't escape from memory. The memory that my work has come to a fortuitous end just as the war approaches its final crisis. The memory of the accident itself. These three nights, which have dragged like as many centuries, I have relived it, step by step, image by image: a series of sharp, visual images strung together by blindly logical circumstance.

Four American women, with a Frenchwoman in nurse's uniform, their guide, are descending from the train at Epernay, where they are met by a French officer. Plump, pink, smiling, the officer. They have come for an afternoon's drive to Rheims and the American battle-fields of the Marne, and will return to Paris *via* Château-Thierry in the evening.

Ravaged fields, shapeless villages.... Soon the Lieutenant has stopped the motor by a steep hillside. The battle-field of Mont-Bligny, very important in the defence of Rheims. He warns us that it has not been "cleaned up;" that we must touch nothing unless we are sure of its nature.

The ladies stream up and across the field, littered indeed with all sorts of obscene rubbish. Some one finds a German prayer-book. Some one else an Italian helmet. There may be a skull in it, warns the Lieutenant; but hangs a French one on his own arm for me. Mademoiselle has a queer-looking object a series of perpendicular tubes set in a half-circle, with a white string hanging down at either end. The inside of a German gas-mask, she says. We all walk across the hilltop as far as the holes dug in the ground by the forward French sentries; we look toward the German lines beyond—then turn back along the crest of the hill, where it drops off sheer to a wide valley. The Lieutenant, Mademoiselle, and I are ahead, the others some fifteen yards behind. Suddenly the officer notes what Mademoiselle is carrying:

"Put that on the ground, please," he says curtly. "I am not sure what it is."

A stunning report, a blinding flash, and I am precipitated down the bank, hearing, it seems, as I go the Lieutenant's shriek of horror:

"My arm, my arm has been carried away!"

I lift my head at once: two women cowering with pale faces, then running toward the road; the third standing quiet by a stark, swollen figure—the Frenchwoman, stretched on her back, with her blue veils tossed about her. Great gashes of red in the blue.

"Macabre of the movies" and aloud I hear a voice, which is mine, add:

"She is dead."

"Yes.... Terrible."

I seem oddly unable to get up. Ringing in my ears. Faintness. The effect of the explosion. Very tiresome, not to be able to help. I crawl farther down the hill to get away from blood. But something warm is running down my own face. Blood! I sit up and take out of the handbag still on my arm a pocket-mirror. Half a dozen small wounds in my left cheek. Unimportant. But my eyes fall casually on my feet, extended before me. Blood! Thick and purplish, oozing slowly out of jagged holes in my heavy English shoes and gaiters. I seem to be wounded. Queer, because no pain. I call to one of the women. She makes a meteoric appearance, tells me I am splashed with blood from the dead; is gone again. I must, I think, lie down. The chauffeurs seem to be above me on the hill now, carrying the officer away. A long interval. They are bending over me.

"Can you walk?"

"I'll try."

It doesn't work. So they make a chair with their arms. One of them is grumbling that the other women aren't on hand.

"Les blésses sont plus intéressants que les morts—the wounded are more interesting than the dead," he remarks.

From my "chair" I note more objects, innumerable objects similar to the one that exploded, straggling like octopi in different parts of the field. The soldiers grin when, in a voice of warning, I point them out. Hand-grenades, they say. Now we have reached the first limousine. The officer is propped on the right half of the back seat, his bloody sleeve (not empty yet) hanging at his side. I am lifted in beside him, my shoes removed, my feet placed on the folding seat. Those nice, expensive brown wool stockings from "Old England" ruined....

The chauffeurs refuse to wait for the other ladies. Must find hospital at once. Unpleasant sensation of severing all connections with the friendly world. Inhuman country. Badly rutted roads. The officer, quite conscious, desperately worried:

"I did tell them not to touch anything, didn't I, Mademoiselle? They'll break me for this." Repeated again and again. Also the reply, "It wasn't your fault, Monsieur."

A bleak barrack at last. An amazed *"major,"* who sticks his head into the bloody car. But can do nothing for us. Gas hospital, this. Surgeons eight kilometres farther on. I feel pain at last and the Lieutenant is suffering. But we talk a little—about his wife, and his profession of teacher.

Will I write to his wife to-night for him? Say he is not so badly hurt....

Dusk already. Two more dreary barracks in a plain, lean and grey. Another French doctor, black-bearded and dour. Very displeased to see both of us, especially the woman. Two stretchers. The Lieutenant disappears in one direction while I am carried into the *triage* and dumped on the ground. To be tagged, I suppose, like the wounded I have seen in the attacks of the last year. At least twenty Frenchmen lounging in this barn-like place. Orderlies, stretcher-bearers, wounded soldiers, all pleasantly thrilled.

"We must cut off your clothes, Madame."

"Bien, monsieur."

I can be dry too. But if there were the least kindness in his grim eyes, I should tell him how desolated I feel to be giving so much trouble in a place where I know it as well as he—women are superfluous.

Compound fracture of both ankles. Flesh wounds from *éclats*. A little soldier writes out a *fiche* in a deliberate hand while I am being bandaged, and given ante-tetanus serum. The *fiche* goes in a brown envelope, pinned on my breast as I lie on the stretcher.

"Is it serious, Monsieur?"

"The left foot, yes, very."

"Can I not make connections with the rest of my party, so as to send a message to Paris?"

No, the chauffeurs had gone already. I am to be sent to a hospital near Fismes. And the stretcher proceeds to the door. Stygian darkness now. As the men slide me into the lower regions of the ambulance I look up and see, peering down from the top layer, the very white, rolling eyeballs of two very black Senegalian negroes.

"You thought you'd be alone?" remarks the dry surgical voice. "No... *Bon voyage, madame."*

The ambulance door seems hermetically closed. How the engine groans on the hills.... How heavily the black men breathe above me.... How my foot thumps.... How the hammering on the wheels pounds in my head when we break down.

Another lighted *triage. I* am lying on another mud floor, surrounded again by men, men. Perhaps I am the only woman in the world.... But the atmosphere is more friendly. An orderly approaches:

"You have three compatriots here."

"American soldiers?"

"American nurses."

Were ever such blessed words? And the tall, sure, white-veiled woman who comes in to take my hand, and not reproach me for my sex, seems to divine just how I feel. *Croix de Guerre,* with palm—Mayo graduate—can this be the nurse who lived so long in a cellar at Soissons, nursing American soldiers? I put her in a Red Cross article months ago! A presence to inspire instant confidence.

"Only a bed in a *poilu* tent," she apologizes. "Impossible to make a *woman* comfortable."

The bed is grateful. Long, long wait. Finally a surgeon with a woman assistant materialize beside me. Surgeon with red face and shabby uniform, and, as bandages unroll, a troubled look. He says immediate operation is necessary.

Miss Bullard confides me to an orderly, Mercier. She cannot see me again to-night. Must prepare two hundred new arrivals, *blesses* of yesterday's attack, for operation. Mercier seems kind. To be brought out of ether by an *ex-coiffeur* is normal, after all this. When the stretcher-bearers come he helps them lift me; wraps blankets about my bloody and exiguous clothing. He says he ought not to leave his ward, but he comes along beside the stretcher, snubbing the *brancardiers,* who are lower in the hospital hierarchy than *infirmiers,* as I have already discovered. The movement of the stretcher on these human shoulders is soothing, though. And the rain that falls on my face from the black night. Too bad to leave it for the lighted X-ray room, so narrow and stuffy, and full of perspiring men. They can't even find the *éclats*. I point out where they must be. Long wait on the floor. At last the summons to the operating-room.

The surgeon is ready. In a white blouse, with a large black pipe in his mouth. He removes it to caution the men who are lifting me on to the table:

"Voyons, voyons! Don't you see it is a *woman?"* A true Gaul. Unable not to point the ruthless fact.

I turn my eyes to the green-painted ceiling. It is spotted with black, black like the surgeon's pipe. Flies. The assistant ties my hands to the table. (In peace-time, I reflect, they wait till one is unconscious.) The surgeon is bending over my wounds now, shaking his head, and his next phrase has no double meaning, and his voice no irony:

"All because a foolish woman wanted a little souvenir of this great, great war... "

I am getting ether in large quantities. Sensation of vibration—of waves beating, and through it voices very clear:

"Who is she?"

"A journalist."...

The tent again. Blackness, clammy chill, penetrating pain. Mercier's hands smell strong of cigarettes. Kind Mercier, washing my face very tenderly...

October 23

THEY are going to evacuate me by the noon train to-day, with a lot of other wounded. The surgeon says my progress is sufficiently good and of course my bed is needed. He has been in to give me special recommendations for the American surgeon (whoever he may be) who will next have me in charge.

This is less of a *toubib,* as the *poilus* call the army surgeons, than I thought. He may look, with his arms bared to the elbow, and his scrubby beard, and his scrubby clothes, like a caricature by Gus Bofa. But he has spared no pains for me, and Gallic to the last has packed my injured members in the whole hospital stock of peerless and priceless absorbent cotton. He has left the small wounds on my face alone:

"Can you suppose I would touch anything so delicate as the face of a woman?"

I am leaving with a dominant sense of the fascination of surgical technique. As so often in the past, my mind has come to life and helped largely in saving my nerve. The limitations of this plant are greater than those of any similar American hospital I have seen, except perhaps one field hospital. Its externals are less inviting. But I am inclined to believe that so far as essentials go good workmanship is rather more scrupulously observed here. Certainly the surgeons take a more individual interest in their cases. I have watched the surgeon of this ward—who is not mine—making rounds every day. No detail is too small for his attention, and he has a personal relation with every man. He is visiting the *evacuables* now, urging each one to write back a full account of his journey and progress.

The *medecin-chef* has come to say good-bye. I was not mistaken in thinking him the operatic tenor of the hospital. He stands at the foot of my bed holding one of his numerous *"paperasseries"* poised before him, like a sheet of music—an order from M. Clemenceau, urging that all consideration be given me. With that in my hand I am to be descended from the train near Vincennes, at the regulating station for Paris wounded. "The *regulateur* will have made all arrangements." I wonder? I have been able to communicate with nobody. And now I must leave Miss Bullard, my rock of safety, my friend, and journey away alone on a stretcher. I don't want to go.

Miss Bullard has dressed me in more of her garments (my own completely demolished) even to a scarf, that was her mother's, about my head. Gertrude's fur coat on top. The brown envelope, with records inside, again pinned to my chest. Great bustle in the ward. The orderlies are assisting the departing *blesses* into their tattered uniforms and tying up their war treasures—such as the *fleas* that have been removed from their wounds. They are very particular about the exact number, and I am not at all in fashion not to have kept mine.

Mercier presents a last tin plate of soup. He insists gruffly that I have been no trouble, no trouble at all. The sun is slanting on the tent floor for the first time; the stove swallows its own smoke. The little *poilu* opposite is better. His face is less pinched, his eyes several sizes smaller. He has reached the stage of patience. He looks on me as a sort of friend now, though we have never exchanged a word, and I feel as if he were reproaching me for going off to a better fate than his. I can't myself believe that these twenty-three men, whose tragedy and comedy—not much comedy, but that of a rich Rabelaisian flavor—have been mine for four days and nights are no longer to be the very core of my life. I can't believe that this tent, which at first seemed so sordid, and now seems so sheltering, will soon be only a brownish dot in the distant "war zone." I *don't* want to go.

On the train

I AM actually enjoying the adventure. Such a golden October afternoon. Its warmth and the vanishing pictures of the country-side I catch through the window of the corridor have given me a new breath of life.

When it comes to the point, I like having to put through something hard alone. Alone! That is one of the charms. For the first time since I left Paris I am by myself—my stretcher on the seat of an old first-class compartment. Only once in a while does the train orderly rather superior personage; antidote to the train doctor who is eminently an inferior personage—come in with a brown teapot to talk of his wife in Montreal.

The train is in no hurry to get to Paris. It is wandering hither and yon, to pick up wounded, and makes long, long stops. We are still in the midst of devastation but I am spared most of it, for from my stretcher my eyes hit just below the skyline. A row of yellow beech trees. Three French soldiers perched on a village roof, hammering and laughing in the sun. Now an elemental figure projected against the blue heaven—a peasant woman ploughing. Ploughing through hand-grenades and unexploded shells. The season of mists and mellow fruitfulness will have its way even here. Perhaps the war *is* nearly over.

The war. What does it mean? Had I even a glimmer of its significance all this past year when I was writing about it, before it really got under my skin?

***

"Unreal as a moving-picture show," an American editor said to me last week, of his recent first journey to the front. That is the way it looked to me when I first visited the Oise and Aisne and Somme only an October ago. The limestone twelfth-century ruins of Tracy-le-Val, overgrown with bright flowers, had a beauty not unlike that of Delphi. Tragedy, but of the Greek order. Tragedy one could regard with a certain detachment. On this last disastrous journey I had to force myself to look out of the motor at the skeleton villages of the Marne. They seared my eyes. Parched my understanding. Every splinter of masonry had a human implication. The dead loss to civilization was past bearing.

Knowledge of war has come by a gradual absorbent process, a sort of slow penetration with its dark background. As it affected the French nation primarily. And especially my French friends in Paris.

Their lives at first seemed surprisingly normal. But gradually these lives came to appear subtly distorted, as faces are distorted by a poor mirror or by a hidden fear. And their spirits: when their once so vital and humane spirits were not full of sinister images they were empty, as the streets were empty during those drab, dragging months that preceded the German spring offensive. The months during which the growing numbers of Americans in the Y.M.C.A. and the Red Cross were discovering the restaurants, and taking war like the rain.

***

What was war to the A.E.F.? In the beginning "a great game," played with wharves, and freight yards, and storehouses, and ice-plants. A great game: I shall never forget the spur to hope that pricked me during my journey from one end of our army to the other in the early months of this year; the sense I got of the constructive force that moved it. But the end of March changed all that. For America only less than for France war then became a drama: intense, vibrant, lurid. A drama that went on steadily in one's own inside, whatever one's superficial activity, and that might well have a tragic ending.

Not like Greek tragedy any longer. And the front and the rear are continuous. Refugees, Red Cross men dashing back and forth from their posts, fighters on leave, wounded; the big gun, the raids, the fleeing industries and banks—Paris is now the war zone. America is at Cantigny on one side, at Belleau Wood on the other. Paris is Germany's objective. Paris is ourselves. Paris is the heart of America, as well as the heart of France.

Paris is saved. But the war goes on. Deeply and yet more deeply is America involved. Not in her brains only—in her flesh. In the flesh, above all, of those tall, sinewy young men in the twenties, who swing so smartly and so sternly down the Champs Elysees on July 4th. Those young men who should be the future of our country. Our finest. If one begins to know now what war means, this is the reason. Sympathy for French or British never brought quite this look into American faces. All the girls who are caring for French orphans and refugees feel they must nurse; pour out their life blood, too, in night watches; steel their nerves too, by holding firmly the ghastly mutilated limbs. Their former chauffeurs and farmers are their brothers; their children. Dearer, because so helpless, and bereft, and in pain.

***

How soon will Stewart and Rick be lying on hospital cots, or worse? Where are they at this moment? The blind query, intensified since my accident, has been gnawing at my consciousness these two months past; since the little Anglo-American lieutenant of twenty—so much more philosophical than the tall American lieutenant of twenty-seven—disappeared toward the British lines after our walk in *vieux Paris;* and the radiant Californian treated me to a last lunch at the Ritz before Saint-Mihiel. Both great lovers of life and of France. Both fully expecting to die some fine morning, "doing a definite thing for no very concrete reason," as the American put it. Both taking a simple and immense pride in their dead comrades, a pride devoid of heroics. In the war they are fighting there is no place for either oratory or vindictiveness. "I have never wasted ten minutes hating the Germans," says Rick. The British lieutenant hasn't either. But he has lost, as the American has not, all zest for war in itself. He envies his American cousins their faith and enthusiasm, goes back to the front with a rather wistful serenity. While the Californian is passionately longing to achieve his aviator destiny.

***

This generation of the twenties has been the important one, in every country, since 1914. Its reactions to war are rawly honest, not befogged by convention, like those of older men. And Harvard, and Yale, and Princeton, and California, feel just as much need to talk and write them out as Oxford, and Cambridge, and the Sorbonne, and the Ecole Normale have done. In the last year I have learned a good deal about how the tremendous business looks to half a dozen very diverse young Americans. To Ernest, doing his responsible job in the rear of the A.E.F.; to Tom, at his governmental post in Paris; to two or three Red Cross men; to Rick at the front. Rick at Saint-Mihiel, in the Argonne, flight commander of a bombardment squadron, sending letters from the thick of the only war activity that has any romance left.

“If I come out of it,” he writes me, “I shall look back on it as the only reality amidst all the pale mirages of experience I have known. There *is* no experience possible wherein man is not at grips with ultimate fate. The only contrast is the contrast of life with death, and the only living making nothing of life. I seem unable to stay out of the air here. If I miss a raid I am wretched until my turn comes again. I don’t seem to know myself. I am neither a hero nor a degenerate. I have found no new surprise in Archies; only a new slant on an old subject in real war flying. And yet my whole state of being has shot up like a rocket. I am having (I suppose literally) *the* time of my life. That is the final consolation to death in battle. It doesn’t much matter what happens once the climax comes. The men I saw go down in flames yesterday were friends of mine. I knew it. Even that didn’t matter. It’s the *damnedest* thing.”

I am not to be persuaded that love of adventure makes war good, any more than the spirit of sacrifice, or the patient endurance of pain. Is it good for the world, for his mother, or for the boy himself, who is so gifted for life, that Rick should be killed? And for how many individuals of the millions of fighters has this war, after all, been good? To prolong it by one unnecessary day, hour, minute, would be criminally wrong—of that, at least, I am sure, after the evacuation tent.

Like the soldier, I feel no bitterness and very little surprise at my individual lot. At every stage I have said to myself: “So this is what it is like”—to drive from hospital to hospital, for instance; or to lie on the floor interminably while indifferent people walk about and brush your face with a foot or a skirt. Certainly I did not want to be hurt. But I have still less right than the soldier to complain. Voluntarily, for the sake of my profession I ran a risk—slight it seemed—and luck was against me.

Mine is no more than a pin-point of sharp experience in the vast catastrophe. Yet its stab unites me to millions of other human beings. To the little *poilu* of the hospital who, under other circumstances, might have accepted a franc for carrying my bag across a platform. *Unanimisnze...* what potency it has. It is that which keeps war going. Every American in Europe to-day, however bad his fate, feels in his heart of hearts glad to be here. Glad not to miss the great adventure of the years 1914-18. For whether war be good or bad, whether it means purgation or damnation for civilization, it is still the adventure of these years. And if one shares, why not up to the hilt? Why not pay the piper?

There my logic fails. I am willing to pay—perhaps; I don't yet know how heavy the price.

But not to let others. Not the little *poilu*. Not the man with no face. Nothing must happen to Ernest, far from his wife and baby. The war must end before Mary loses her second son. Before Rick goes down in flames.

Dark now. And I am suddenly terribly tired. The hard stretcher has eaten its way into the very marrow of my back. The doctor takes my temperature with a frown. Says we shan't arrive before ten o'clock—ten hours' journey. He has had too much *pinard*. So has the orderly. I have a sneaking hope that somebody somehow knows I am coming. If only, oh if only I might find an American face—Gertrude's? Ernest's?—on the platform....

American Hospital of Paris, Neuilly

October 24

I AM reincarnated. As a perfect lady, in a perfect sick-room, full of flowers. Flowers after Mont-Notre-Dame. And the peace of being alone within four spotless, grey-white walls. Fresh white curtains, white cushions, white furniture. A long French window into a garden. October tree traceries—black and gold and purple, like Versailles—against the sky. A bell-rope, the genius of which is a beautiful young Alsatian girl in blue and white, who brings lemonade made of real lemons that quench fever; tea on a tray with dainty strips of toast; ungreasy bouillon; eggs refined to custard; hot-water bags which yield to pressure instead of repelling it. I wonder if cantankerous souls exist who think this hospital a prison?

I have been in a state of exaltation ever since Colonel Lambert got my stretcher out of the ambulance, well after midnight, and down the white corridor which ended in a white bed—with pillows! A night-nurse with melting Portuguese eyes. A middle-aged surgeon in a dressing-gown. A hypodermic. This was Neuilly. Blissful haven.

Much good M. Clemenceau's recommendation did me, though. I still hear the grey-beard of a regulating officer ranting over me in the hospital tent at the station, while I tried to hold on to my self-control and my wits. (High fever and great pain by that time.) Ranting because he did not know where to send me; because the ambulance boys hadn't come. The hour they took in coming...

And the face that peered into the little window of the ambulance from the driver's seat when the "boys" deserted me in the velvet blackness in front of the Hotel de France et Choiseul. "An *apache,*" I thought. On the contrary, the poor old literary night-watchman, blubbering over my hand, nearly in his emotion tolling the bell that roused us so often for raids to give notice that here I was again. Several sympathetic shades of my dead life collected about the ambulance, as it was. And the Colonel, spruce and good-humored in spite of the hour, climbed in and sat himself down on the other stretcher, as if for our usual war gossip. How many times did he say, "I'll be damned" on the way to Neuilly. For once I made the Colonel sit up.

The whole of my previous existence in wartime Paris returned with a rush this morning; as normally as if the sealed world of Mont-Notre-Dame, the world bounded wholly by pain and death, the world where only wounds and *poilus* existed, had never been. But for that slowly winding train, which somehow linked the two together (how often have I similarly readjusted my universe between Boston and New York!) I should be dazed to find myself once more in the midst of war-rumor, political discussion, and familiar entities like the Y.M.C.A., the A.R.C., and the A.E.F. It was the blue and grey "Y" that came dashing in first, in the person of Gertrude; red cheeks, solicitous eyes sparkling through her glasses, armfuls of fruit and flowers, and stores of her rarer gifts of high spirits, generosity and humorous human interest. And then the steel-grey Red Cross, personified in R. M., with her warm, wise smile and limitless capacity and kindness. Both assuming my responsibilities, reinforcing friendship with the power of these great organizations that I have spent so much time studying and criticising. (Glad I am now always to have maintained that their virtues outweigh their deficiencies.)

Then came along the men, Lippmann and Merz, Arthur Ruhl, Tom, and others, all equally human and concerned. The New Republicans also shoulder my responsibilities, and I am ashamed to remember that I once thought W. L. a cold intellectual. My stoicism would certainly ebb away from contact with this flood of friendliness and flowers, if every one were not so obviously relieved, especially the men, to find me not a nervous wreck. The crisis is very near, they think. I must get to work again. In fact I have engaged a stenographer for next week. If convalescent *poilus* make bead chains in bed, why should I not string words together?

My little blue-and-white nurse reproves me for writing to-night. Perhaps I am tired, for the doughboy voices from the garden disturb me. It is my heart, not my nerves, that the A.E.F. troubles. The garden holds a Red Cross tent hospital, an overflow from "Number One," the big Ambulance in the boulevard Inkermann. The wounded—in khaki here—are hobbling by my window, on crutches mostly, to their supper. Rattle of tin plates. End of a lighted tent projecting into my field of vision. It is unjust that I should be enjoying daintiness and luxury, under a real roof, while soldiers are outside where rain can drip and stoves smoke. And the worst of it is that it will soon seem natural that I should be here and they there.

October 25

MY fate as a *bless&* is in the hands of an American surgeon of remote French descent, who appears to be even more of a Francophile than I am. A Southerner, with very Gallic airs, and almost Provencal loquacity. I already know much of his family history—great surgical family. *Grandpere* volunteered under Napoleon and made the retreat from Moscow; *pere,* Deputy-Surgeon General of South in Civil War. He himself volunteered in the French Army at the beginning of the war, and served three years before transferring to the A.E.F. He operates half the day here, and half at "Number One." He has a casual manner, jollies the pretty little nurses in a Franco-American jargon of his own (good accent, though). He would like me better if I would only laugh at his jokes or cry pathetically while being dressed. I can barely preserve a stony silence. He handles my wounds like a connoisseur, not to say a lover of wounds.

I can't altogether cheat myself into thinking I have returned to the old world, though. Not so long as I have a daily dressing. The intensity of apprehension I feel when the surgical cart is wheeled in, and my bed wheeled out, and the surgical nurse begins to undo things, humiliates me. For I do not believe in the importance of physical pain—until my leg is lifted out of the splint. Then I don't believe in anything else. Dr. M. cheerfully tells me to yell. He says the difference between French and American wounded is that the Frenchmen howl, but keep their arms and legs still, and the Americans mutely sweat, but wriggle in all directions. He congratulates me on the work of the French surgeon who, it seems, did a very skilful job in saving the left foot at all. That information sends a cold shiver to my uttermost parts.

October 28

THE face of the world changed again. I am to have the wounded soldier's experience, *jusqu'au bout*. Infection in left foot. It set in on Friday evening. The work I imagined myself beginning to-day is remote. Virtue has been trickling out of me, and fever and pain flowing in. How did I ever write at the other hospital, on the train? All I care about now is quiet. And air, fresh, cold air; because I feel stifled and contaminated. And a nurse, a quiet nurse, always there. R. M. has sent one; fair, pink-cheeked, shy, slow, steady. A Norwegian Red Cross nurse, from a North Dakota farm, just landed; the very antithesis of the quick, sophisticated little French pupil nurses who have been in and out like humming-birds.

Visitors eliminated. I couldn't even talk to Ernest when he came hastening up from Dijon yesterday. I couldn't even bear the sound of his voice. But the affection in his eyes sustains me yet. (Fine, frank, judicious brown eyes.) That is something I dare let down the bars of stoicism to—family affection. More sustenance there than in the rather dubious words of Colonel Blake, whom Colonel Lambert brought in consultation this morning. (Shall I lose my foot yet?) Our most distinguished American surgeon looks the part, with a becoming greyness. Acts it, too. Dr. Pd., whose *"specialite"* seems to be always to be somewhere else when demanded, failed to turn up on time.

I have just had my first irrigation with Dakin solution, through two Carrel tubes in my left foot. Now I know how *that* feels, too. I little thought, when I accepted Dr. Flexner's invitation to hear Dr. Carrel lecture on this great contribution to modern surgery at the Rockefeller Institute, that those lurid Pathe pictures of wounds would soon have such a personal import. May my wounds heal with the miraculous rapidity which Carrel described!

At best it will be a slow business. Hospital till January at least. The doctor told me the first morning that I should eventually walk comfortably "on a level." My face must have fallen, for he inquired, with a twinkling glance at my many bandages, whether I was an Alpinist. Couldn't I make ascensions by funicular? I have been haunted ever since by the fear that I may never climb Page Hill, Chocorua, or High Pasture, Dublin, again. I am just as much in need as ever of their wild, sweet, junipery flavor and their spacious views. No more different because a hand-grenade has hit me than Rick is different because he has dropped bombs on Germans.

October 30

I WAS wrong. Rick is changed. Not by dropping bombs, probably. By his brother's death, and the decimating battle of a month ago. Grey and stern he looked as he stalked in. Scarcely a flicker of his happy young smile. Moving heavily instead of with his usual light case.

He sat down in the corner of the room farthest from my bed, and regarded me broodingly, out of eyes black in their sockets. Not as if he were sorry for me. Not as if it were odd that I should be in bed with wounds and broken bones, and he intact. Rather, aggrieved. As if this were just one straw too much.

The rest of his reconstituted squadron has gone to Nice on leave. He doesn't like the new men. Couldn't stand that sort of thing anyhow, just now. But he counted on my being as usual, more than usual, perhaps, a sympathetic ear, a safe family friend, a literary comrade—some one to see him through. And I am of no use. (He didn't say it, any more than the *poilu* at the hospital said it, but he looked the same reproach.) I can't even eat a meal with him. I elicited the fact that he is eating alone, at the Cafe de Paris. Why the Cafe de Paris? Not like you. No. That's it. Because he never ate there with P. c. R. or the other eight friends who were blotted out at the end of September. He couldn't go to Voisin's because it was there that he found his observer eating that historic gourmand's lunch—tended by six waiters holding the choicest wines of the *cave* in their arms. Nor could he go—well, anywhere. He is paying in one large lump for all the leaves (and especially the A.W.O.L.'s) he has taken here in the last year.

Were they all killed, the men he lost? Probably some prisoners. The ghastly part is that he lost track of them for about fifteen minutes, when his plane was out of control. His observer—who was his closest friend—shot dead, fell on the rear controls, and he could only steer blindly into Germany, pursued by twelve Boches with forty-eight machine guns. When he came to, there was just one of his six planes behind him. The young pilot was going across for the first time. Wonderful pluck, the way he stuck to Rick's tail. That was what got Rick back again. (He never admits his own bravery.) Now young P. has been lost, too. He must go to see the family in Paris. It seems that he does nothing but look up the families—or write to them....

How many times have you been shot down? Three. Never a scratch. He showed me, hanging on his wrist, one of the bullets that embedded itself in the plank under his feet on September 26th. The plane was a total wreck.

He has received answers from my cables to his family. His mother has been splendid. (Tough luck to lose B. Tough for the boy not to have got to France. To die in a camp of pneumonia. He can't talk of that.) She says he is not to try to get released on her account. So he will go back to the front. Go back soon. Paris is a graveyard.

The doctor had allowed my visitor five minutes. But how shall I send him away if he gets any dim comfort here; sitting on in the corner, tilted on two legs of the stiff chair, his long, straight, powerful profile, ending in a jaw two sizes too big, outlined against the grey wall. Rain-in-the-Face. He might just as well have his aviator's helmet drawn over his head. For there is where he is: at the front. He is quite unaware of the effort I have to make to drag my voice out of the depths of my head. He is sunk in trouble; completely immersed in that intense and violent world whence he has come.

It seems impossible to write his mother a cheerful letter, as I have done after his other visits to Paris. How should I write of anything but war as I see it now? War choking itself out in spasmodic breaths through dank nights in hospital tents. Faces blackening into death. Fine, straight young limbs turned rigid. And why should Rick get through, even now, though such a natural adventurer? The zest is gone, and that may be just enough to turn the scales of his luck. There is no reason why he shouldn't be killed on the last day, in the last hour.

Finally he gets up. Lights a Fatima abstractedly. Says he has a taxi eating its head off out there. Sticks on a jaunty cap. Shakes his broad shoulders in his smart, French-cut uniform. Gives a faint flicker of a smile. Avoids shaking hands. But stops at the door an instant and looks at me with a sudden hope. Perhaps I have a panacea? No, there she is, ill in bed. Wounded. For one second he seems to take that in as it affects me. Hastily extinguishes the Fatima. Then he flickers again, and is gone. Back to the front.

PAX IN BELLO

November

STILLNESS. Intense stillness. Try as I will to throw it off, it muffles my bed like a heavy blanket. Or like one of those mosquito bars that smother you in Italian hotel bedrooms. I lie underneath, on my back. Always on my back. Immovable and straight. Holding my ears rigidly clear of the pillows—listening. No sound. No faintest echo of this glowing gala night. Only stillness, soft, spongy, clinging. Stifling me in its pale web.

The garden, all I can see of it by turning my head very gently to the right—I must not stir by a hair's breadth that distant part of my bed where my aching feet abide—is full of white moonlight. The black trees that frame the clustered tents are spattered and silvered with it. Hoary old trees. Safe Red Cross tents, with eyes of yellow light that twinkle boldly to the lady who floats aloft. Two months ago the moon gathered bombers as an arc-lamp gathers moths. A thing of dread. And now how large, and round, and clear she sails. And what soft security she floods upon our garden. This is the fifteen hundred and sixty-first day of the war. After fifteen hundred and sixty-one days the women of the world may go to bed with quiet hearts.

My heart isn't quiet. It is pounding and throbbing under the bedclothes like one of those airplane motors that are always disturbing the air of Neuilly when I most long for peace. I wish I could hear an airplane now. It is desperately still. If the doughboy who twangs the wretched banjo that daily jars through my pain were only marooned in the garden. I would give any three soldiers five francs each to start a row.... Not a sound. Every patient who can hitch himself along on crutches has got into Paris somehow. Armistice night. The culmination of the most terrible four years in the history of the world. The only wounded left, out there in the tents, are like me, tied to a bed. Too ill to do anything but listen. Listen and strain for a celebration we can't hear—and perhaps can't feel. Our war isn't over—as the *femme de menage* put it this morning.

Strange somebody isn't travelling over the Neuilly boulevards. There should be at least one belated taxi with a horn, carrying a smart French colonel just arrived from the front toward Paris. At least one cab, drawn by a tired horse, pounding back with a family of *petits bourgeois* who keep early hours because of the *gosses*.... Utter silence. All day the hospital walls have trembled with the reverberation of great trucks from the munition factories along the Seine. Trucks carrying the French work-people to Paris. Through the double door of my room, which usually deadens hospital movements, I have caught a murmur of suppressed excitement. Nurses' voices raised above the usual careful level. White shoes pattering at the double-quick. The surgeon, urging the young ladies in his warm Southern manner to hurry along and *Pier la victoire*. When he came to do my dressing he was very impatient to be gone himself. (His face looked worn above his white gown. He isn't altogether glad the war is over, I surmise. More surgeon than humanitarian. And not very keen to leave his bone-grafts at "Number One" and his Paris nights for private practice in a sleepy, stolid Southern city.) Hours since I've heard the least twitter in the corridor. As deserted as the garden and the street. If I thought it would make a sharp, strident sound, I would lift my left hand and squeeze the bell that is pinned to the bed near my left ear. But it only lights a small, red, silent electric flame, they tell me. What's the use?

Dr. M. promised me a bottle of champagne to drink to victory. It didn't come. Miss O., my Red Cross nurse, was more disappointed than I. She "had never tasted champagne," and glowed at the wicked prospect. Rather dismally, at last, she tucked in the extra pillows, my only substitute for a change of position through the night, and wondered whether the trams had stopped running. She, too, wanted to get away from wounds and pain. To see and touch this Paris gaiety of which she had heard so much in North Dakota, and scarcely dared open her eyes to when she arrived. Poor boulevard sights. No, I couldn't have drunk to victory with some one who did not know what Paris was like last June, when the Germans were only forty miles away. And champagne is a mild stimulant by comparison with this pain of mine. A black, misty, mounting flood which sweeps me off, tosses me back and forth like a cork on its tide.

ıng and swirling do not muddle my head. Somehow they ever did my senses feel so acute. If one of the wounded ›uld get up and dress (eluding his night-nurse), and drag hı...self over to the iron fence that shuts in our garden, and whisper to a little French girl through the bars, I should surely hear her answering: "I loove you." Yes. But there isn't even a lover's whisper in the clear, crisp, empty air that comes through the window. The little French girls have forgotten the wounded doughboys. They are in the "centre," dancing around laughing, drunken, vociferous, rich American officers—generals' aides and quartermaster captains—on the once-more lighted boulevards. What pictures swim before me. If I can't hear I can at least see....

Rainy French ports. Mellow old French cities. Barren French villages—all full of olive-drab, brown-faced Americans, celebrating the Armistice. Dazed they must feel in the mud of our Camps, the manufactured cheer of our canteens, the high efficiency of our railway centres. Just so much stage scenery now. But the hospitals are not stage scenery. Base 15. Savenay. Evacuation Hospital Number One bitter reality. I see a wounded soldier with hollow Lincoln eyes, and a lantern jaw. He has a hole in his abdomen. He is crying for water.... *What is it like at Mont-Notre-Dame to-night?*

The *petit chasseur* breaks in on my visions: it is only at this evening hour, when my nurse is gone, that he dare thrust his clipped, Boutet de Monvel head, with its impishly demure round face, inside my door. A big envelope with the Embassy stamp. Out of it this huge proclamation, which was placarded over all the walls of Paris this morning:

REPUBLIQUE FRANCAISE CONSEIL MUNICIPAL DE PARIS HABITANTS DE PARIS

C'est la Victoire, la Victoire triomphale; sur tous les fronts l'ennemi vaincu a depose les armes, le sang va cesser de couler.

Que Paris sorte de la fiere reserve qui lui a valu l'admiration du monde.

Let us give full course to our joy and our enthusiasm, and force back our tears.

To bear witness of our infinite gratitude to our great Soldiers and their unconquerable Leaders, let us decorate all our houses with the French colors and those of our dear Allies.

Our dead may sleep in peace: the sublime sacrifice that they have made of their lives to the future of the race, and the safety of the *Patrie* will not be sterile.

For them, as for us, “the day of glory has come.”

LONG LIVE THE REPUBLIC! LONG LIVE IMMORTAL FRANCE!

To it Tom, the thoughtful sender, has appended a P.S.:

“Long live immortal France.” But don’t regret your remoteness from the “day of glory.” Paris is not nearly as grand as during those epic days and nights of endurance just before ChAteau-Thierry. I cannot see the end of the greatest war in the history of the world, and the greatest ordeal that France ever withstood, in the light of a football rally. I should like to talk to Cesar Franck to-night and hear him play stately, towering symphonies. Or to stand on the height, with Sainte Genevieve, very late, after the turmoil has subsided.

Looking down, under a chill, unemotional, watchful moon, over Paris, city of cities, asleep.

All very well for Tom to talk in this magnificent vein. He is there, in the midst of the turmoil. If he really hates it so much, why did he not come out instead of sending a messenger? This is the first day since I reached the hospital—more than three weeks ago—that I have had no visitors. Natural. But depressing to be alone and detached on a day of collective emotion.... Tom is right, all the same, about the grandeur of the days of trial. They come back to me, one by one, scenes in a picture-show far more real, more immediate than the stifling peace of this night.

The second day of the March offensive. The big gun has been aimed at the heart of France for twenty-four hours. Paris has already established an attitude—the attitude that bombardment is a thunder-shower, whose lightnings usually strike amiss. Crowds on the boulevards, taxis circulating, sad faces, tense faces, absent faces, but never a shadow of fear.

B. B., hurrying from the Red Cross to lunch, stops to buy a paper from the old woman at the kiosk opposite the Madeleine.

"Bonjour, madame. I haven't heard that famous gun of yours for at least half an hour—have you?"

"Que voulez-vous, monsieur? Faut qu'il de-jeune!—It has to have its lunch."

***

The Portuguese night nurse looks at me oddly. I must have laughed aloud. She thinks I am wandering. She was in town this afternoon, and still wears a dreamy look that matches a rose tucked in her belt. She tells me, with her shy smile, to rest, as she attaches the long rubber tube and turns the cock that sends a cold flood of Dakin solution through my bandages. *Rest!* Paris haunts me, too.

I address questions, persistently, obstinately, to the dim blue-and-white figure moving about my room. *Have they taken away the last of the sandbags that muffled the fountains and statues so deeply as the spring wore on? And the last of the decorative strips of paper that were supposed to save plate-glass windows from shock?* (The rue de la Paix went in for diamond patterns, the Champs Elysees ran to cubism—even the toy-shop window on the rue Saint-Honore sported strange, geometrical beasts.) *What has become of those delightful yellow balloons which rose into the pale sky after sunset?* Their cords were to entangle the tails of the swooping German planes. One might think Paris were coquetting with war... but for the faces.

Absent faces. The crash of the "Bertha"* brought them back to the scene they were ignoring with a sort of quiver. Faces. *What did you read on the faces to-night, Mademoiselle?*

**A long-range German siege gun.*

No answer. She is gone. Only stillness, stifling me in its pale web. Those April nights, nights of the offensive, the stillness was even more profound than now. Even more stifling. A breathless hush that brought the battle close, close, close.

Suddenly, corkscrewing into an unquiet dream, the siren. French guns. Another *alerte.* The cellar? *Ca manque de charme,* as the stolid chambermaid says. I will stay in bed. But the concierge is ruthless. He goes on ringing a huge bell that hangs just outside my window. He bangs at my door. The Swiss head waiter, shrieking, *"A la cavel a la cave!"* has turned out all the lights before I get downstairs, and dives before me into subterranean regions that date from an ancient convent.

In the first *cave* the sports of the hotel are already uncorking champagne; in the second, a Spanish scene—a card-table with one flickering candle, a lady in black evening dress and three swarthy, masculine faces; in the fourth, the cowards, maids and valets of every nationality gloomily whispering; in the last, brightly lighted with electricity, the *beau monde.* Trying to look as if it were their custom to spend the night entombed in a seven-foot vault lined with dusty bottles of old wine.

Mr. Ford, of the American Red Cross, protected by Mrs. Ford, has all his valuable papers under his Louis XV chair. He is making notes for his stenographer. The other males, though British officers, are less Olympian; in the tilt of their expressionless heads against the unyielding stone walls one divines a secret grievance: wives have decreed this ignominy.... The red-haired refugee from Russia, with her Bowery accent, her three-year-old boy and her sixteen-year-old French nurse, take up a great deal of room. So does Mrs. de Peyster's Russian wolf-hound. His mistress, with her pearls about her neck and her diamonds in her wristbag, summons M. le directeur to demand a carpet for the next occasion. Mrs. Thompson, in her green sweater, also finds it impossible to make her Chow comfortable. He has to yield his gilt chair to Miss Ames, who has slipped a fur coat over a gorgeous dressing-gown that belies her uniform hat. She has come from her canteen at the front—where they arc bombed every night—for a quiet night in Paris. The prettiest of last season's *debutantes* puts up with a pathetic little stool.

Boom-m-m-m-m—

"Oh, do you suppose that was the Grand Paiais? I wish we could hear more, don't you? The only thing that I don't like about this cellar is that it muffles everything."

"Couchez, Chow! *Couchez tout a fait!* Mrs. de Peyster, do you mind keeping your dog the other side? *Tout a fait,* Chow! I am a little nervous—not about bombs. This is such a small room for a fight. I don't mean on your *lap*. We do love to treat them like children, don't we?"

"How discouraging! I had heard to-day from somebody who really knows that things were better in Washington. Oh, no, my dear; it was a Major who told me. Well, anyhow, Baker is in this raid—I hope he heard that one...."

"What does that waiter want, snooping around?"

"They have sent him to see that we don't take any wine. Ten bottles disappeared last time."

"John, John! Did you see where my husband went?"

"Yes, they say it was a German General in

British uniform who ordered them back...." "Waiter, please go up and get me a glass—I want some mineral water. You don't think I ought to ask him to go up? But you know as well as I do that man is a German spy if any of his old bombs drop in our court...."

I steal out and climb the stairs. The sharp sound of the explosions is dying away. The French cannonading has stopped. Soon the *berloque* will announce the end. I stick my head out of my high window. Utter blackness, blackness that denies the very possibility of light. Yet through it, on the street below, is already travelling something warm and vibrant and human: the Paris crowd. It is as if a river, obstructed for a moment, had found its normal course again. The murmur is slightly subdued, confused, but eddies of easy laughter, voices disputing as to where the last bomb fell, float up to me. Here come the bells—blessed bells, sober bells. Nobody who has not heard them tolling peace, tolling sleep, through the solemn nights, knows the fortitude of the soul of France.

Not a bell, to-night. I will call the little nurse and ask her what Victory has done to the soul of France, that Neuilly broods over it so glumly. No. She would not understand. I must just keep on remembering, and remembering.

June... The shadow of a new sound haunts the silent small hours. Something like a heart-beat, a heart-beat of the night itself, or like a breath, a sighing breath, shaking me in my bed. (So, during the Marne, they say, could Paris hear the guns of the front.)

In this breath American guns at last have their share. Travelling through the darkness toward Neuilly in our ambulances come our young veterans, armless, eyeless, choking with gas and blood, exactly as the veterans of Mons and Verdun have come before them.... The sound gradually ebbs away. A crack of daylight—I open my curtain. The *garcon de cafe* opposite has paused in his white-aproned rolling-up of iron shutters to read the *Matin*. A working-girl passes with her nose in a paper. Next an old gentleman in grey spats, and an American private—both lost in the news. "Better or worse?" How can I help shrieking down from my fifth floor: "Is it worse or better?"

"Plutot mieux," answers Charles, bringing my roll and jam. "We have counter-attacked." What right have I to rolls and jam?

Never was such intense and exquisite weather. The air is gold and light, the sky brilliantly soft and blue, the sun burning hot on the wooden pavements, the shadow of the grey arcades along the rue de Rivoli cool as crystal. The grey-green spring with its delicate yellow flowers has turned into glowing summer. Red roses on *midinettes'* breasts to tempt the American soldier; red roses at the street corners, red strawberries and cherries on pushcarts. Women with carmine lips buying pink collars at the stalls outside the Galeries and foolish little dolls to charm off the Gothas—Nenette and Rintintin. Red taxis laden to the roof with luggage; Red Cross flags, Red Cross uniforms, Red Cross trucks. Outside the headquarters the latter stand in rows—full of packing-cases, full of nurses; as doctors distribute gas-masks, the truck drivers read *Paris-Midi. Are they any nearer?* Again every passer-by is lost in a journal. Even the privates of the Signal Corps, playing baseball in the noon hour in the

Tuileries Gardens, stop sometimes to take a look at *The Stars and Stripes.* The *demoiselles de niagasin,* sitting on spidery iron chairs and eating their lunch out of paper packages, comment admiringly on these broad-shouldered sweethearts, who occasionally dart up to proffer a greeting in argot.

"Pretty much at home," says Bob, just back from the front, as he leads the way toward the best restaurant on the Champs Elysees.

Yes, we Americans are pretty much at home in Paris now. We have a right here. There is no condescension in the accent of the *maitre d'hotel* at the Restaurant des Ambassadeurs.

"Melon, sir? Sturgeon, sir?—one only gets it two or three times a year, sir."

Bob orders melon, sturgeon, and champagne. Outside the hedge that shelters this perfection, the chestnut trees and the benches, where fluffy children used to watch Mr. Punch and lovely ladies used to preen their parasols, are sprayed with dust from heavy military *camions.* The young persons who sit on the benches now are tawdry, the babies who play about are grimy little refugees. From the windows of hotels and great houses loom the bandaged heads of the wounded. Luckily, Bob does not look through the green barrier. He carried one of his men three miles on his back yesterday—but he does not tell me that. He gazes blissfully at the spotless cloth, at the red roses and red awnings, and he yields up his hundred francs with a murmur of praise for the arts of Paris. But just as we start a woman thrusts *La Liberte* through the hedge. The Marines are attacking....

L'Intransigeant, La Liberte—another raucous, breathless newspaper hour, the hour of the afternoon *communiqué.* The people on the boulevards 1 63 walk like inchworms, digesting a paragraph with every inch. Nobody speaks—*they have advanced a little....*

Night is here again. Or rather the long, blooming summer twilight that lasts till half-past ten. Over the strident sounds and colors and anxieties of the day it drops like balm, drops from a soft grey sky shot with rose and yellow, bathing the Seine and its springing bridges, brooding over the nobly massed roof-line of the Louvre,

Blooming on the gardens, where sculptured trees and tender nudes blend their *genres* in a rapt dream of beauty. In the dream, sharing it, walk France and America—together, and not alien. Yet there is a private standing alone. What does he see? A stone basin, an obelisk, an arch with a sharp sliver of new moon above it. Arizona taking the measure of Napoleon! Can Arizona save Paris? Must these lovely stones—fragile as Venetian glass they look to our eyes to-night—be sacrificed in the process?

"If need be," says Tom, who sits on the bench beside me, staring at the empty spaces in the fading light. Taking account of the incisive meaning of Paris in French and world psychology. He has lived with the Germans in Brussels—he knows what it would be to see them here. What does this new brand of young American not know about Europe—many things, certainly, that Henry James and Whistler never learned through years of eager application. More "Europeanized," though they don't realize it, than the self-conscious " Europeanized" of the old days, who cultivated sophistication and a French accent at the Beaux-Arts. The new type has a right to speak of the destinies of Europe. *Paris must not be taken.*

Darkness falls. The long vista to the Arc de Triomphe is pricked with peacock green and orange—the stage is set for a raid. _In another half-hour the heavens will be alive with light and the shrubberies cracking with shrapnel. The translucent screen of beauty that has interposed itself for an hour between us and the front again turns plate glass. Out of the night comes the voice of a French interpreter talking with an American friend: " Peace? Buy an inglorious peace with Paris—can Germany believe it? Athens was destroyed, Florence was devastated by the Spaniards and her beautiful ring of encircling villas razed to the ground. History repeats itself. We should have no joy in our houses, in our Louvre, in our Notre Dame if to save them we had to consent to peace. But how we shall love them, Colonel—or what remains of them—if a noble battle waged by your troops and ours together saves them for us...."

***

The Portuguese night-nurse is bending over me again with the same shy, troubled smile. "Your hypo."—thank Heaven! This effort to reconstruct the past keeps my heart going too fast. My American friends will not Sainte Genevieve include them in her protective meditation to-night, up there on her blue height? Americans who have become bone of the bone of Europe, through sharing so intimately in her agony. Men and women both, they have a stake here now. Few of them will be able to go back to their old lives on the old terms.

Queer. I can't remember their names. I can't see their faces. I am floating out into a region where only shadows exist. Misty and dark.

Sounds. I hear something at last. A horn. A taxi horn. And louder, vaguer, denser echoes—like the roar of New York. The celebration is reaching Neuilly. No. It must be the universe, roaring in my ears. A universe freed from the bonds of war. Whirling madly in the dark. But there was the moon, distilling peace and security in our garden. Stiffly I turn my head. She is gone. In the garden, too, only the whirling dark....

November 12 A WONDERFUL sunny morning. Miss O. wears a white uniform by way of celebration—instead of the ugly grey one the Red Cross invented for its foreign service and fresh, and pink, and happy it makes her look. (There must have been a letter from her North Dakota "man" last night.) She opens the French window wide upon the garden while I eat my breakfast, and lets "Saint Martin's summer" in. Just outside a very pretty tableau: some of the wounded boys stole a captured trench-mortar from the place de la Concorde and dragged it all the way to "Nooly" in the small hours. Now they are painting it, with a grandly possessive air, while French and American flags are collected for a procession.

Morning is the easiest and most normal time in a hospital bed. Because the busiest. The number of commonplace duties to be got through gives an illusion of useful living. Everything is an event: having one's temperature taken, having one's wounds irrigated; sponge-bath, fresh linen (luxuries I fully appreciate after the French tent), two minutes with Miss G., the assistant head-nurse, whose skin is always creamy, whose blue eyes are always jolly, however early she makes her rounds. Even the *femme de menage* is an event.

When the whistles and bells began to announce the signing, at eleven o'clock yesterday morning, the *femme de menage* was on her knees scrubbing my floor. Sharply she lifted her broad, brown, peasant face. Pushed back her straggling grey hair with two dripping red hands. Then leaned her great bare arms on the rim of her pail. Rested there, looking toward my pillow, an expression of slow and poignant beatitude spreading over her seamed cheeks, till even the deep-set corners of her eyes and lips were trembling with it.

"C'est la paix, madame.. mon garcon... sauvé...."

Two tears rolled down into the pail.

"C'est la joie. Depuis si longtemps qu'on a *éte ferme..."*

It is so long that we have been *closed*. Yes.... Suddenly our hearts are wide open. Full of something bright to incandescence—the flame of all the lives that will no longer be snuffed out. Mont-Notre-Dame... Rick... Stewart.... It must be that those boys are safe. It *must* be.

Still the robust old woman leaned her arms and her heavy breast against the pail, looking at the American propped on her pillows.

"But the war isn't ended for Madame. Nor for all those poor soldiers who, like Madame, were wounded toward the last. (They won't get the same care that the others did. In the tramways already people don't get up to give the *mail&* their seats.) Nor for me, the war isn't over. No... I lost my other son at the Chemin des Dames. The twin of this one. Cleverer, he was. And the cost of living going up. Hm... *oui.. oui.... C'est comme ca, leur maudite guerre."*

The last phrase rolled up from the voluminous depths of her skirts in the rich, lusty voice that adds Voltairian commentary to her morning's scrubbings. She had found her normal self again. And her normal quarrel with society. *Leur maudite guerre*. "Theirs," not "ours." Theirs, the government, the bourgeois, the rich. We fought it, her tone implied, because we must, and because indeed we couldn't have the Boches marching in. But we are realists. We demand now, why you, you the rich and powerful and intelligent, did not find some less disastrous method of saving us and yourselves?

Against me Madame Mangin (no relation of the general, she wishes me to know) bears no grudge. I have suffered. And Miss O. and I do not treat her just as an obstruction to the floor.

"Mademoiselle is good," she says to me every day of my nurse, and would teach her French in return for this human decency if Miss O. were not too shy to venture a word. Madame Mangin is Miss O.'s first experience of class distinction and class degradation. On her self-respecting North Dakota farm to scrub was part of the day's work. She is profoundly shocked by the subjection of this generic French army in patched blue gingham, which steals into the hospital at 7 A.M. and glides over every inch of the floor space on meek knees before noon pushing its pails out of the way of the scornful white shoes of the nurses, and the cursing military boots of the medical staff.

Madame Mangin is very conversational this morning as she swabs my linoleum. Recounts how she and her daughter—an old maid, more's the pity—celebrated the Armistice with cousins near the Bastille. Whispers that the Monsieur in the next room is "more rich than poor. He has a rug. And an open fire!" Laments that butter is getting scarce. Fears that her son will have difficulty in finding a job. Her son has, nevertheless, had advantages. For lack of them she has had to do hard manual work all her life. An orphan, she was. Brought up on a farm by public charity. Placed in service. Married to a day laborer, who became paralyzed and was fifteen years in dying. A year after his death her two sons are taken by the army. One returns...

"What does Victory mean to me, Madame?"

"Monsieur and Madame A. S.," announces Miss O.

The *femme de menage* reverts to type, slops her way humbly out of the door, as the visitors come in. They are delighted with the childish tableau of the doughboys and their trench-mortar. Madame has brought fruit and jelly for the invalid. And it is characteristic of the poet's sympathetic kindness to be the first before any American friend, as it happens—to cheer me with a description of Armistice Day. His blue eyes are like a summer river, reflecting one delicious image after another. This writer of the grey-gold beard and the subtle intelligence loves to brush elbows with his humblest fellows, to smell their dirt and sweat, savor their racy jokes. *"Je suis tres, tres populaire, vous savez, tres democrate,* very much of the people." And yesterday! All his disillusions about the war were swamped by the great wave of joy that overwhelmed the Paris streets.

What a sense he gave me of the beloved city suddenly translated from its drab war-sadness; suddenly all brilliant flags, white armistice streamers, embracing people, variegated soldiers and processions—especially processions which formed in one kaleidoscopic pattern, dissolved, formed in another pattern. From every grey street and square, they emerged, spontaneously generated: French school-boys in long, singing columns, dragging enormous guns after them. American and British soldiers in huge motor trucks, workmen in blouses, employees of the "Samaritaine" or the "Bon Marche," with banners; housewives; refugee children in uniform guarded by Sisters of Charity. A. S. used an expression similar to Madame Mangin's—something about a closed vessel suddenly opened to sun and air and happiness. Absolutely natural and right, he thinks, the demonstration, and adequate because it gushed up from the tired and sad old town like a fountain of new life.

His great interest after processions was in individuals. He and Madame S., who was sustaining his enthusiasm like the good French wife she is, kept interrupting each other to describe this or that person:

"Do you remember the old concierge who had certainly never emerged from her lodge since 1870, as she wore, Mademoiselle, exactly the clothes of the period..." it. She was leading a group of school-children—that was the queer part—hobbling ahead of them, beating her crooked old arms to make them sing the *Marseillaise: "Allez, chantez la républiquel'"*

"And the washerwoman, with a basket on her arm, who said to A. on a street-corner: 'Everybody is happy—I, too, am happy for the *patrie*. Yet I remain all alone.'"

"And the one-legged *mutile* who stumped ahead of three or four rows of wheeled chairs pushed by Red Cross nurses, calling: 'Make way for the *embusques!*'"

"Yes, Mademoiselle. And they were singing, those poor fellows, in chorus:

"Mourir pour la patrie,

C'est le sort le plus beau."

"The crowd was absolutely silent as they passed. Suddenly a woman in black rushed forward holding out both arms—but before she reached the first *mutile,* she stopped with a gesture I shall never forget and *took off her hat.* Then, holding it clasped to her breast, she walked down the line kissing each man on both cheeks."

"Beautiful," said the poet, wiping his eyes.

***

Later

A STRING of callers. As I lie here alone I wait impatiently for their coming. But as soon as my grey room and my quiet are invaded I long to be again remote. Remote and immobile on my high bed. Not obliged to move even a muscle—or a lip. Like a mediaeval lady carved on a stone tomb. Such a lady with her hair in two braids over her ears—must have fretted when she heard the French Revolution raging outside her dusky cathedral nave. Yet when the stained glass was shattered, and voices poured in on rifts of light, she, too, would have cringed...

For instance: at the sound of the peace bells the American Red Cross thronged to the place de la Concorde. There, while French mothers—how many thousands of them—were praying, it executed a snake-dance, under the leadership of some of its most famous "majors." This was reported by Mary, with no *arriere-pensee* as to the suitability of serpentining, as she removed laundry and jam for my comfort from her flowered bag. I don't know what I should do without this gently cheerful little visitor who came, as usual, in her lunch-hour, with her blue veil and cape over her nurse's aide's uniform. Then hurried back to her ward: heavy convoys of American wounded have been arriving since last night at the Ambulance. Terrible, inconceivable as it seems, one of our divisions in the Argonne *attacked yesterday morning...*

The psychology of these gentle, passionate, well-bred, brown-haired American spinsters who, after two or three years of nursing—nursing gas and wounds, in hospitals sometimes bombed and shelled—yet take pleasure in the street celebration, amazes me. Elizabeth, my second visitor of the species, was glorying besides in the harshness of the Armistice terms. As I think it over, she, who nursed largely in Belgium, is the only hater—not excepting the French pupil nurses—I have seen. The only person thinking about Germany's humiliation as the reverse of our triumph. S.'s joy in the streets was not that: it was joy in the world's—especially the French common people's—liberation.

Tom, who appeared next with Vernon Kellogg, had felt no joy at all, but was bent on amusing. As by the story of the French soldier who was tearing along so full of enthusiasm that he inadvertently collided with a horse. And, nothing daunted, clasped the animal fervently, shouting: *"Vivent les chevaux!"*

I suppose I laughed now and then. Though what I was chiefly aware of was the niceness of these two busy Hooverites journeying out here to provide eyes for the *blessee*. Tom looking distracted—the Food Administration plus the C.R.B. drive him hard. Pale, too. When I first knew him, last year, in the Red Cross, he was rosy enough to live up to his college nickname. And had a childlike and disarming smile. The bureaucrats of French food are doing their best to make him look like a worried old man. As for V. K.—who also belongs to the Napoleon-race, for stature, and is surely something of a genius—he, too, is flogging his energies with his nerves.

Well—interesting to note that every nation reports its own people—the Americans made the town hot. Seized taxi-cabs, put *abri* signs on them, piled inside and on the roof, and drove down the boulevards blowing horns and shooting off revolvers, to the amazement, if not the disgust, of the natives. Took complete possession of the Café de Paris, threw out first the waiters, then the *gendarmes,* rifled the *cave,* kept on the lights and guzzled till two in the morning. Tom had an encounter with one drunken Captain who asked him to buy for him (as he "didn't speak the d—d frog-language") an American flag from a passing taxi-driver. The French chauffeur refused to sell. The Captain offered fifty francs. No, not at any price. The Captain insisted, with fury, that an "American officer" must naturally have a prior right to "his own flag." And when Tom said he certainly couldn't buy this one, roared out: "I believe you're nothing but a d—d frog yourself!"

Of course, our compatriots went in strong for *midinettes.* Tom said one of his finest impressions was in a side-street off the boulevard des Capucines, where a triumphant voice issued from the dark: "I got a girl, 'Erb, come on!" And a friend of his achieved success by addressing every good-looking lady in best American-French: *"Mademoiselle, la guerre n'est pas encore finie." "Comment, pas encore finie?" "Non, it faut donner un dernier coup"*—whereupon an embrace!

The celebration, they explained, was very limited in area, limited almost to the boulevards. To drive down the Champs Elysees and the rue de Rivoli was to feel on the outward fringe—close enough to get the throb and thrill, yet apart. The centre of the thrill was the place de l'Opera which, viewed from a tall building near by, "was like a great swarm of far-off people engaged in some gigantic demonstration" which attained dignity and even mystic grandeur in the blue afternoon mist.

Dr. Kellogg reports that his wife has started for Lille and Belgium. (To think—I might have been with her.) He is off to Poland. I wonder if this professor of biology will ever go back to his laboratory? Far afield he has wandered. And Tom—who hopes Hoover will soon liberate him from Paris for something more adventurous—what is to become of him? If he had not gone to Belgium from his college sociology, he might take his place as a "young Radical" in the office of some New York journal. But now—how can he use his thoroughly aroused will-to-power and his first-hand knowledge of the inner springs and devious routes of European economics?

***

All the visitors gone, at last. Queer to call up the reflection of the Armistice celebration in their varying temperaments, as the grey dusk thickens, and the black fog of my pain. Take Tom's reaction. He hated the festivities. They offended his artistic sense. Tarnished the greatness of the hour. Only perfect silence could have satisfied him. But, humanly speaking, he thought it entirely decent for the A.E.F. to yell and get drunk, and indulge its appetites. While Major E., of the American Friends' Unit, suffered the most intense shame to see American officers chinning themselves on the gold chandeliers of the Café de Paris. Swilling champagne, running so much more amuck than the other Allied officers "who had suffered so much more in the war." Major E. saw I was sailing into a dusky region. Set down his big basket of hothouse fruit with quiet sympathy. If not so roused would have liked to tell me pretty stories—one about a sailor boy in the rue de la Paix who fell out of his procession and "shinnied" up a fluted column to Paquin's balcony, to get a kiss in return for a rose. *Midi-nettes?* There this very unmajorly major faltered, almost blushed. New experience in his sober life to kiss his way out of a circle of laughing, painted girls. "Garden of Eden conditions," he apologized—"not at all what it would seem at home..."

As for Walter Lippmann,* who turned up with a cloudy look last of all, probably he did not even see the street-scenes. What he saw was President Wilson's face, thrown on a screen above the great crowd in the place de l'Opera. A face greeted with enormous emotion—cheered far beyond those of Clemenceau and Lloyd George—by a crowd preponderantly French. The severity of the Armistice terms is dire for Germany, W. L. believes. Still more so for the Allies. He had been reading Gauvain in the *Journal des Debats,* who significantly points out, to-night, that the Armistice "makes no allusion to the Fourteen Points;" and that the President's peace programme is purely theoretical, "must now be developed in conformity with circumstances." If this is the tone of a very liberal authority, Wilson must surely come to France.

**Walter Lippmann (1889–1974) Famous American writer, reporter, and political commentator.*

***

No use. The pain detaches me from politics.

From my bed. Hurls me out into feverish space with a queer sense of home-coming. I seem to belong in this vague sphere. Subconsciously I wait for it, long for it. That is why I am so impatient when I have to fix my attention on daylight commonplaces. Why I find it so difficult to talk and listen. In this dimmer region is truth, glimmering. Always eluding me. But glimmering ahead.

To-night I see faces. Rick's face. Long and thin and black under the eyes—as it gets when he is thinking instead of flying. He believes the great crisis of his life is behind him. Believes he has drawn a blank. Is amazed to contemplate the fact of mere existence. Poor boy. I wish he would send me a telegram. But an intuition will be all I have to go on till some day he saunters in....

Ernest: he will have been drinking to victory in some tapestry-hung salon of the *noblesse* of Dijon. And when he gets back to his humble billet he will pause, as he begins to remove his huge military boots—wrinkling his nose characteristically—to wonder what he is to do and what Katharine and Nancy are to do with the series of aesthetic and leisurely reactions on life, the taste for old wines and rare etchings, the love of the French humanities, the French tongue, and the French race that he has suddenly substituted for the hard drive of a law office in a rather barren Middle-Western city.

And Lucinda: Her delicate, dark face and great brown eyes so much more lovely and tender than when I first knew her a year ago—are bending over her wounded privates at Dr. Blake's. Convoy after convoy pouring in.... (When will she come to see me?) She has discovered her heart and her energy for the first time, in nursing. Can she go back to a conventional New York life?

Gertrude: in a Y.M.C.A. hut crammed to the roof with the First Division, making a tremendous speech about peace. Eager listening soldiers who drink up her vitality and her unselfish ardor. The sort of understanding of variously average American men that she has acquired—what will she do with it now? And how will she do without their enormous reliance upon her, their need of her ultimate power of giving?

What is to become of all of us? We might have been in a closed sack for four years. A giant hand has unloosed the string that binds it. Tossed us free into space where we sprawl and kick and choke, because we have so much air to breathe. Surprised, aghast. Michelangelo should be here to paint us in these catastrophic attitudes.

November 16

FRESH, clear, snappy morning. Almost like New England. The Red Cross nurses, passing my window early on the way to duty in the tents, huddle under their blue capes lined with red. The boys limp by to breakfast more briskly than usual. An aroma of American bacon makes me homesick for my journeys up and down the A.E.F.

No more swift, cold drives in khaki-colored cars. No more marvellous American growths springing from the ancient French countryside. Impossible to realize that the Armistice guns have shattered the A.E.F. into bits. It had come to seem imperishable, a living creation. Yet the millions of men who made it live will soon be spread wide over the vast surface of the United States. Lost again in our grinding industrial cities, our tin-roofed Western farms, our barren New England villages. I am forever asking myself what traces they will keep of their contact with Europe. They will all be marked, in one way or another. A good many will be lightly powdered with French earth. But only a few will find roots clinging to them; roots that will shrivel or weep a European sap when inserted into the soil of Indiana or Maine.

Maine—wasn't that where the first body of American soldiers I ever saw in France hailed from? The ones I happened upon in a lean, brown, pastoral country that might itself have been Maine. I had just come from Verdun; from the still beleaguered citadel, from a land sternly organized and scarred by war, and swarming with seasoned French troops. Then all at once here was the A.E.F. The first squad was drawn up for drill in a poor little peaceful, brown-tiled village. Service hats, that made them somehow look like Pilgrim Fathers, set squarely above red cheeks. Next, with unaccustomed helmets sliding at a rakish, almost a girlish angle, came a machine-gun company convoying one lone machine gun along a wood road. In the willowy valleys, and on the piney hillside, sparse groups of infantry. Could anything so innocent and unequipped as this trans-Atlantic force of ours ever become an army trained to the 1918 arena?

Ships landed without docks. Warehouses built without wood. Stores transported without cars—one learned of the fibre of America in a journey from the Base ports to the Lorraine front! Carolina stevedores singing at their unloading in the crowded harbor of Saint-Nazaire. Negroes building railroad tracks (I saw three in Civil War uniforms) in sandy central France. Boys from Pennsylvania shunting freight cars—"Say, you have to talk to this engine in French, or she won't go!" East Side Jews and Italians building depots. Foresters from the Pacific cutting and sawing for the Italians. Southern engineers building bridges. Cowboys from Colorado tying their mules in turreted French villages. Men from Minnesota sitting up in hospital cots "Northwest of Toul" to describe in German-American the Boches they had done for.

And then those masses of khaki I walked into by the Madeleine one listless July night when hope was low. A line of motor-trucks extending as far down the dingy, deserted boulevard as the eye could reach, loaded with American guns, American supplies, American soldiers. Inexhaustible resources, inexhaustible vitality! Tears rise to the eyes of the quiet French population that gathers quickly out of the twilight. The American boys have such jolly, comical faces, so burned and ruddy, so black with dust, and with roses stuck in their hats and their rifles.

"At any moment may descend hot death. To shatter limbs! Pulp, tear, blast Beloved soldiers who love rough life and breath Not less for dying faithful to the last."

Beloved soldiers, beloved *Americains*. Glasses and bottles are whisked out of cafes. Pretty little street girls swarming like bees, offering roses and kisses, charming in the sense they have yes, they, too, have fine French feelings, these little girls—of the fine young American faith offered to save France. *"Les chers enfants, les braves, qu'ils viennent de loin"*—yes, we were the only child-hearted people left in this racked and disillusioned Europe last July and we came from far, far "to tell the world." That was our greatest contribution to the Allied cause. We are young yet after the Argonne and the Armistice, and now we are going far, far back again....

"Those poor boys think they're going to get home for Christmas," says Miss O. from the window. "I just wish they could—they're more restless already."

It's true. There is something in the faces even of this small circle of wounded survivors, still dressed in unified olive-drab, still moved by group emotion, reading Pershing's "Victory order" in the *Herald*, that shows a relaxation of the patient common purpose of the A.E.F. A new sort of discontent. The next months will in certain ways be harder than the war, more of a strain on morale. Pershing does well to sound a warning as to the dangers of victory. Petain sounded it first. His order is the finer, for the French tongue lends itself to the expression of high emotion:

History will celebrate the tenacity and the proud energy spent during these four years by our country which had to conquer in order not to die.... You will not reply to the crimes which have been committed by a violence that might in the excess of your resentment seem legitimate.... Having conquered your adversary by force of arms you will further dominate him by the dignity of your attitude; and the world will not know which to admire more, your bearing in success or your heroism in combat....

I wish Petain had not used the word "crimes." Why not, since crimes there were? Perhaps one wants the Allies too magnanimous to underline their magnanimity. Perhaps, when one has seen war at close quarters, words of civil justice lose their meaning. I was still pondering these questions, this afternoon, when Miss O. brought in a quasi-official French visitor—who, as it happens, had talked to me a great deal in the past about German "crimes." Madame S., with whom last year, when she was acting as press guide for the French Government in the war zone, I journeyed to Alsace and Verdun. She was eminently fitted for the job from the official standpoint: well born and bred (the daughter of a distinguished Academician and novelist), flexible in talk, agreeable to travel with. Convinced of the necessity of spreading certain types of French ideas, yet handing them out in such homoeopathic doses that most of the foreign ladies swallowed them quite unsuspecting. Slim and smart enough, too, and quite hard-headed enough to make a soft, feminine charm, rather than a masculine grip, her stock-in-trade—especially with the French Army. No sinecure to persuade an *officier de carriere* to be receptive to American women journalists! I have a genuine *sympathie* for her, and she one for me, I believe, though she mistrusts my New Republicanism as I mistrust her Catholic conservatism and her undefined, but very definite, foothold in the inner temple of French diplomacy.

She came to-day to inquire for my wounds in the interest of the Quai d'Orsay. By the time she had praised my roses, and astutely criticised my chrysanthemums a bunch of gorgeous hothouse blooms—for their "coldness," she had taken it in that I was accepting the fortunes of war without thought of blame. Whereupon she plunged into politics.

To Madame S. November 11th equals triumph over Germany. *On les a!* It sparkled in her black eyes (eyes quite wickedly pretty even on ordinary days), gave her pencilled lips a special curve of vindictiveness, added *verve* to her delicate, bird-like gestures. The Armistice terms, she thinks, are duly hard. She is by no means convinced that France should not extend her boundaries to the left bank of the Rhine. M. Berthelot is drawing up the statement of France's claims, and he can be trusted. Germany is defeated: surely it is legitimate and natural that this stupendous fact should dominate the French intelligence just now. Yet there was something ominous about Madame S.'s exultation, as she spoke of the Rhine, the flight of the Crown Prince to Holland, the abdication of Charles of Austria. Not the joy of a democrat in the democratic future of

Europe. President Wilson's probable coming she mentioned with a certain reserve—the tone of the *Debats* and the *Temps* as contrasted with the frank joy of *l'Humanite*. But she believed that once he had visited the devastated regions he could not fail to realize...

She, too, had been in the Paris streets on the day of the Armistice:

"I found myself in the crowd between two wounded officers. Chasseurs Alpins they were. One of them, a Captain, had such an attractive face that I asked him if he were feeling happy. `Yes, we're glad of victory. But what grieves us, my friend and me, is not to have been able to stay at the front to the end. Only a month ago that we were wounded. No luck!'

Then she told the story of a marquis, the owner of a great estate north of Verdun, who arrived there in his officer's uniform on November 11th before the Germans had gone, to the alarm of the tenants:

"Attention, M. le marquis, les Bodies sont kir "Don't worry, my good friends"—and he retired triumphantly to sleep in his dog kennels, leaving the Germans in his house for a last unhappy night.

Chasseurs Alpins and marquises: a very different France, hers, from that of the poet's republican vignettes. Madame S. paints her country much as the charming French officers who came to America in the spring of 1917 represented her to us, in a glamour of horizon blue. I shall always have a weakness for horizon blue. But I can't be too thankful that I never wrote, under Madame S.'s guidance, the sort of propagandist article approved by the "Affaires Etrangeres." In her heart she respects me for not having done it, though she regards "propaganda" as entirely legitimate.

Propaganda!—whether German, British, French, or American, it appears to me a giant bugbear, sitting hard on the chest of the world. I am so depressed by a glance at the censored evening papers after Madame's departure that my nurse suggests a chapter from Willa Cather's new novel, "My Antonia." She loves the book herself, for it takes her back to the farm, and the villages she drives to over the treeless, windy roads of North Dakota. And I, through the magic of these very simple words, lose myself, too, in blond corn-fields; in miles of copper-red grass drowned in fierce sunlight; in a free, frank, grassy country which, as the author says, "seems to be running."... I see it " running " from the Franco-American spells evolved by the complex brains of the rue François Ier.

How inaccessible to such spells—if the complex brains only knew—are Americans like this placid girl sitting beside me. (Thousands of American soldiers of her species.) She descends from the blond, isolated corn-fields as I descend from nubbly New England pastures overlooking the sea—the sea that washes Europe. The sea that keeps the tongues of Latin Europe haunting in my ears, and throws a mirage of its storied cities before my eyes. Nothing in Miss O. washes, reflects Europe; at least Latin Europe. If she strikes a self-respecting course through the dark mysteries of Neuilly, that is due to sheer character. Such character as her Norwegian father showed in guiding his prairie-schooner into the Dakotan wilds. Duty is her guiding-star—duty to me whom she admirably accepts as "her patient," though she made a real sacrifice to come across plain and ocean to France to nurse wounded soldiers. I have ever so many more points of contact with the little French nurses who do things for me during her hours off—yet, have I? It rests me enormously just now to see her sitting there, cosily, in her ugly grey sweater. As impermeable to the subtleties of my late visitor as one of those nice, friendly prairie-dogs, beloved of Antonia.

Always the vibration between wanting visitors to give me vicarious life and knowledge again, and hating them because they hurt my still peace. Each new figure in the pattern of my days tinkles sharply against my silence and my pain—as a bit of colored glass drops into its place in a kaleidoscope. But by evening suffering and pattern merge. And I am fused with both.

Sunday, November 17

FRENCH gentlemen have got out their high hats to-day for the first time since 1914. In honor of the first official celebration of Victory. An Alsace-Lorraine procession down the Champs Elysees to the statues of Metz and Strasbourg. The cities no longer in mourning. Soon to be entered by the French troops.

Another lonely *fête* for me. But I had one dear visitor, Lucinda. Pale, exhausted, all eyes under that night-blue veil I shall be so sorry, for aesthetic reasons, to have her give up. She looks about at the end of her tether. The climax of her intense effort of service has been reached in these last days—among the worst they have had at Blake's. Mostly men wounded on the 11th itself. She has a patient, a "wonderful boy," *blinded* at ten o'clock that day.

At eleven o'clock on the 11th a number of the hospital staff, nurses and doctors, were gathered in a small room downstairs about the coffin of a much-beloved patient—a boy whom they had tried desperately to save, and who had won all their hearts. The victory guns and bells sounded through his burial service.

Lucinda says that she went to the window afterwards in a sort of daze. She saw people across the way putting out flags. They had "a strange expression on their faces." "As if it wasn't true."

"That's the way I felt myself," said the poor child. For months she has lived—as much as any young infantry officer—with the immense sacrifice, suffering, heroism of the doughboys. She has dressed their shocking wounds, used every resource of her being to bring them back to life, watched by them as they died—died calling for their mothers, calling her "mother." And from this consecration, this sense of the constant company of the dead whose lives are the stuff of "victory," she emerged on Armistice night into streets "like New York on Election Night. No exaltation. No prayer. No knowledge of what I had left in the hospital on any face." Only self-indulgence. Excess. Stupid rejoicing. Drunken officers (always this chorus).

"While the war lasted the excitement and necessity of it kept you going. But now you can't help wondering if it had to be. Why it had to be. Whether the world will be the better for it...."

She looked at me questioningly. But I have no reassurance to offer. Even if I had, this *jeune fille bien elevee*—Lucinda was preeminently the American equivalent of the term a year ago—would not accept it at second-hand, after her months of very fundamental first-hand experience.

Miss O. went to a service to-night and one of the Alsatian sisters got me ready for the sleep that never comes. She had been to the procession—in which the other sister marched in costume—and says the crowds, though very reverential, were also unmanageable. Sweeping away all the "barriers" and making hay of police regulation—to the joy of the American soldiers, perched on guns, statues, and Tuileries tree-tops. The crowd was further harrowed and thrilled by the airplanes, flocks, droves of them that came darting and wheeling down from the Arc de Triomphe, doing the most breathless stunts, to meet clouds and coveys of pigeons set free in the Concorde. All this in the blue November haze with a tinge at the end of sunset gold—the colors of the Paris late autumn and of Puvis de Chavannes " Sainte Genevieve." And afterwards a "Victory Te Deum," celebrated at Notre Dame.

I can forego the procession. But what a hunger I have for those rolling chants, those Gothic spaces, those prayers of anguish and thanksgiving!...

November 18

THE French troops are advancing into Lorraine. They will probably enter Metz to-morrow. In time I shall hear of it from F. T. The *Herald*—so very anti-Wilson—has to-day a patronizing editorial eulogy of our President which ends by insisting, in Madame S.'s manner, on the value of his visit to the devastated regions. I am sure he ought to see them. Yet if these scarcely veiled suggestions that he does not know what the Boche really is like are not dropped, he will feel as rebellious as I do when asked to write a dictated (the French word *tendancieux* has no good English equivalent) article. Arthur Ruhl's account of his visit to Alsace comes back to me: he was so thoroughly and officially "guided" that he got no chance to talk to the natives. Finally he succeeded in dashing alone into a tobacconist's and stammered out to the old woman: "Do you want to belong to Germany or France?" "To neither!" she replied with spirit. That is a story one should not remember just now—for comfort.

November 19

RICK has reappeared. As large as life and twice as casual. Surprised—and sorry—that I have worried about him. Didn't think about wiring or writing, since he was O.K.

He does not retreat to the corner this time. Stands a moment taking me in from his well-balanced height. Remarks dubiously that I look better and "very clean." (He is thinking of the wounded at the front with their ghastly smooched faces.) Then disposes himself astride one of the stiff chairs by my bed.

"Well—here you are—after all—*mon cher.*" A flash of responsive affection from the very depths of his reserve. (Good. He wanted the assurance that I am glad he is alive. Especially as he doesn't know whether to be glad or sorry—for himself.) But his next look hopes I'm aware that this is a rotten anti-climax, after so many heroic farewells to life.

"Now what?"

The light dies out of his voice and his eyes. He is going home—very soon. They will release him on his mother's account. Offered him a job in Paris. What's the point, after the front? Naturally it would be pleasant. Too pleasant. So many pleasant times in Paris in the last two years and a half. Town already not what it was during the war. Of course there's Poland. And Russia. And the Balkans. All sorts of openings for action and adventure—this with a sigh and thickening gloom. Every temptation to stay on and on.

"Don't you do it, Rick. If you go home now, you'll always have the best of the two worlds. If you stay, you'll turn into a rolling stone on both continents. But I realize how hard it's going to be—after so long."

His dark, concentrated gaze inquires whether I *do* realize....

"Have you cabled?"

"'Have survived the war. Please send $500 against return.'" An eighteen-year-old twinkle at the recollection. "That will convince mother. The squadron thought it was a great idea—trying to grind out sentimental family telegrams." On the strength of cheerful reminiscence he takes a comfortable stretch to the iron cross-bar of the bed with his beautiful three-hundred-franc boots. (His are not, alas, the first military boots for which that bar has had a fatal attraction. And the contriteness of the culprit is almost worse than the jar to my fractured ankles.)

"Got the news of the Armistice at the squadron the night before. Picked up by wireless. By the Colonel's orders it was announced at the Y. The officers threw their chairs through the moving-picture screen. The men proceeded to blow up everything in sight. Stole all the bombs and flares, piled them in the road, and set them off by a system of electric wiring—with *terrific* effect. Everybody on the loose. My mechanic accidentally ran into the squadron adjutant. He jumped aside and saluted, but the adjutant yelled, 'To hell with that stuff, the war's over!' The Colonel ended by putting the whole camp under arrest."

The news produced in the flight commander a fierce desire for liquor. Commandeered the Y.M.C.A. Ford and scoured the country. When he got back, though, with a case of champagne, neither lie nor any one else wanted it. The new men, who'd never been "across " and were cheated out of their war, went to bed. The old men sat up—half-heartedly.

"In the morning we listened for the guns. Heard them. Wondered if we'd be sent out. Weren't. Though it was perfect 'flying weather'—pouring rain. We were playing chess at the time hostilities ceased. Somebody gave a whoop. That was all. In the afternoon the Colonel graciously pardoned us. Read a report on the valorous exploits of the squadron...."

At this, gloom thickens again. I am to know that the war came to an end just too soon for my young friend. Recommended for a captaincy. Been promised a squadron of his own. In another month would have been a Major and a C.O.

"Another month!"

A rather wry smile responds to my protesting tone. Oh, well—he didn't get his month. Just as he never got his chance to go out with the French. Did I remember all the months he waited—all the false alarms of orders? And now, after the last disappointment, he went up and did such suicidal acrobatics in a heavy old Breguet that he was nearly put under arrest?

"There could be no heroes—could there?"—he continued after a pause "if man really had a sense of humor. Nothing I undertake seriously but the gods turn it to farce. I give you my word. The war is the biggest farce of all."

***

Why will people stay so long?

That boy haunts me. He is so completely out of a job and sees nothing ahead but moral responsibility—from which he shrinks as much as he courts physical danger. Superficially, the world is his oyster. He takes daily life with delightful ease and buoyancy. He is having a "good time" now. Disporting himself—so far as a clean-minded, vigorous, Western American can—in the elaborate manner prescribed by Paris to drown care. For the conscious or unconscious purpose of ignoring and repressing his doubt of himself.

The doubt that he may not make good in real life as he has made good as a flyer. At heart he knows the worth of his own stuff and mettle. Yet he is afraid that his vaulting ambition will peter out when no longer backed by the violent incentive of risking the neck. Yes, he is seriously out of a job, now it is all over.... And despite his zest for action he has a literary temperament. He never acts but he reacts on his action. On paper. Don't I know? Always plumbing his still waters and adding himself up, especially in his letters. His friendship for me is little more than a peg on which to hang his conclusions. I happen to be near and he must disclose to somebody the black turmoil of his spirit....

Too much responsibility for me as I lie here on this helpless bed. The dark whirls so fast that I can't even get things clear. I have no job to offer him on a silver salver. How shall 1 convince him? Conflicts of peace—they generate the creative impulse as war generates the destructive. He can't stop fighting. He must create.... Write his adventures and his doubts into books. It will need, my friend, the best of your brain and nerve.

November 20

FOR the first time since my arrival, nearly a month ago, I was lifted, just now, on to a stretcher so that my mattress might be turned. To ease the strained, stiff back on which I must continue to lie. Miss M., the kind head-nurse—as Irish and dark as her assistant, Miss G., is Saxon and fair—directed three nurses in the job. They were almost more nervous than I. The horror of having my left foot touched.... On the days of dressings my dread begins long before light.

Again in my fresh, level bed (but they forgot to take out the grinding ache at the bottom) I suddenly realize, as Miss M.'s tired face vanishes out of the door, the weight of responsibility she carries. Realize with compunction how deep in individualism I have sunk, shut up so safe here in my grey cell. I know—and dread—the patient in the next room by her cough which comes hoarsely through the wall. I know the one overhead by the quick, trotting step of her nurse. But all the other horizontal shapes are nebulous. Suddenly their need of medicine, dressings, thermometers, hot-water bags, becomes vivid to me. I wonder do they accept these sacramental hospital attentions as a matter of course or do they marvel—as I, though fallen from the grace of *unanimisme,* still marvel—at this avaricious hoarding and cherishing of the breath of life that so extraordinarily contradicts the squandering of war. They may not think so much as I do about the breath of life. They may be rolled in coma. Or restlessly tossed, like skiffs moored in a stormy harbor.

For me, too little coma. I am always stringing my heart to courage and persistence. It keeps me stern. *"Pauvre aniie,"* said A. S. the other day, *"vous avez un air que je ne connais pas,... un air si severe."*

November 22

ONE great imaginative picture we shall keep of this war that has been so poor in ceremony and circumstance: the surrender of the German fleet. The newspapers are full of it to-day, and even they, with their debased verbal currency; can't cheat the spectacle of its terror and romance and retribution. Watching those German battleships sailing, Indian-file, into the British lines and captivity, I felt for the first time a thrill of victory. Down goes the German Colossus into great dark waters—with a splash that rocks my bed. And as the waters grow calm and blue again the British Empire appears, floating serene on their crest. Gibraltar, Africa, Egypt, India, Australia, Canada—fabulous names, encircling the world. All that Britain has done through the war, her courage and fortitude and inarticulate determination, her very blunders and stupidities, seem compensated by the mastery of the sea this day affirms.

Yet Wilson proposes to change "mastery" into "freedom"—freedom even for the prostrate Colossus. This opens too large a window on the world and the Peace Conference to be comfortable for one's shivering intelligence.

My nurse regrets that I have had no visitor on this "historic" day. I did have one, quite as real as if she had come in flesh and blood from London to sit beside me in the grey afternoon light—so that we might try to puzzle out together, in disjointed fashion, how closely the cooperation of the armies and the fleets which to-day's events substantiated had really linked American and English understanding....

"I am always intensely conscious" (she said) "that Wilson will be the chief figure at the Peace Conference. Practically all Europe and England will have to submit to his dictation—and a great many won't like it! And a certain proportion of the group are the men who best represent what great things a great England has stood for.... They will not respond to his moral idealism where material and practical advantage are concerned any more than they have responded to America's militant ardor during the past year. We in England had suffered too long and too deeply... Yet how lucky that America could generate sufficient ardor to take the wonderful stand she did."

"It was" (I answered) "chiefly with lack of ardor that the American troops reproached the British with whom they were brigaded. They had been trained and nourished in an atmosphere of enthusiasm and they encountered a frost—tea instead of coffee, and a frost."

"Yes" (she replied), "I have been going to a large American hospital twice a week as Red Cross visitor. The men suffer so pluckily—I am melted with appreciation and affection for them. When they get up they drift to us for a cup of tea and fill every nook and cranny of the house with an insidious breeze from America. Their criticism of the familiar type of British officer is racy enough. They vaguely strive to do him a *little* more justice than their prejudices encourage or allow. But the deep and great *entente* of the press hardly assumes more impressive shape than this to the objective eye...."

"Isn't that" (I insisted) "somewhat the fault of the whole British military policy of deliberate separation and detachment? I can't tell you how remote England and the British front have felt to me during this last year in France—almost more so than they felt in America. From the moment I landed in Bordeaux the war as it concerned France and America was interpenetrated, crudely actual; the Franco-American *entente* was a thing of deeds, not words. But the British-American remained vague and ' literary.' Just because the British army—in spite of a certain number of British officers in Paris streets and restaurants—remained physically and psychologically far away, like something written in a 'war-book.'"

"What changed my own feeling" (I went on to say) "was the appearance, toward the end of last July, in the courtyard of the Hotel de France et Choiseul, of a young officer in the uniform of the Royal Field Artillery—a little Anglo-American whom I fancy you know well. (He looked extraordinarily, touchingly young to me, though he bore himself with an easy grace that seemed his natural approach to life.) We sat down together at an iron table. He chose a *benedictine* in the interest of sophistication—though it should have been a *citronnade,* for the day was warm. Then, with a happy, humorous, philosophic smile that recalled his Scotch father—and took me straight back to certain games of Slap Jack into which a carrot-headed, freckled, argumentative little boy of nine put much zest—he began to talk of his rediscovery of America."

Boys in the A.E.F., girls, *such* charming girls, in the A.R.C. Their names were echoes from distant American years, and his interest in them had a gleam of his mother's sensitive appraisals. He was eager, delighted with both America and Paris—with Paris (which he was seeing for the first time) partly because it was so American, and partly because it was so French—so living, so spacious, so very beautiful, so much more than London, he said, the heart of the world and the war. Already he felt that he belonged here: whether rolling like a prince in a taxi-cab up the joyful luxury of the Champs Elysees (following sundry extravagant purchases on the boulevard Haussmann) or eating *en plein air* in Montmartre, with *gosses* after Poulbot begging for sous, broad-hatted, cadaverous types out of Louise stalking by, and M. le Patron, in a little black velvet cap, and an enormous beard, playing on an *espece de guitare*.... His appreciation had a freshness and a nostalgic enchantment that I put down to the American blood in his veins as well as to relief from the front, the rather tiresome front to which he must return when his precious week was over—the *British* front. Before he had finished his little golden glass, it had taken on as sharp and dread an actuality for me as the front where Rick was bombing. In those masses of khaki, in that lurid and booming region shadowed by disaster, I should now see one individual figure—individual yet symbolic of a great risk and a great hope....

****

My friend speaks at last. Or do I just imagine her voice, coming so dim out of the dark?

The Armistice has brought no news of Stewart. He has been missing since the end of September. Fourteen months since he left for France and the same regiment in which his elder brother was killed in the battle of the Somme—left feeling glad that he was old enough to do his part, though he hated war and had the happy, reasonable, harmonious nature, the vital approach to life which seems to hold a key. War was in no sense his destiny, as it had somehow seemed Morton's destiny.

No, whether Stewart comes back or not, I shall never associate him with that grim lunar landscape where his brother—still borne up by the heroic emotion of the first years—met the end that his temperamental restlessness sought and made fitting. Morton belongs in one of those poignant graves, overgrown with straggling roses and tucked about the half-ruined apse of a French Gothic church in some wholly ruined French village of the Somme.

But Stewart—I refuse to connect with tragedy the connoisseur of Château Yquem—"I *always* drink Château Yquem," said he, with an air of initiation which secretly enchanted his beloved trio of girls at the Hotel des Champs Elysees—the host at a *loge* at the Francais—and how he did appreciate the perfect art and tender Gal- lic irony of " Boubour oche"—the companion of my walk in *vieztx Paris*. I shall think of him, rather, as haunting always those beautifully proportioned seventeenth-century rooms of the Musee Carnavalet, which a guardian, drowsing in the July stillness of the courtyard, had the discernment to open for his benefit. Emptied of their treasures since the German advance, they were all the more full of Madame de Sevigne and her friends for that—shades exquisitely welcoming to the *si gentil* and responsive young foreigner; whose answering salutation gave them the assurance they needed—the assurance that it was worth while for an Anglo-Saxon to risk death to save such monuments of the French creative mind as this.... That he faced death lightly indeed, and keenly, without phrases or self-pity, like all the best of his generation.

He talked to me on the way home, I remember, about the French girls—the sort who wear paint and powder and dark circles under their eyes. /Esthetically they were rather displeasing in their pervasiveness, and he had discovered that Americans—in their revolt from Puritan tradition—gave them too much attention. Sometimes one amused one's self by imagining what a Paris leave might be if one found a *nice* French girl to go about with—there *were* nice ones in the number, who would never have chosen that life but for the war.... Still, no relation could be so delightful, so wonderful really, as this he was discovering with American girls of his own kind. There was a freedom, and charm, and equality about it—he wished his sister could know those three girls. So animated, and cordial, and intelligent to talk to, so different from English girls! He was looking forward to the last evening—he had arranged a surprise: when they came up from dinner to the salon, there would be three bouquets, one for each, the best Paris could produce to express his thanks for the way they had taken him into "a home from home."...

I tried before his mother faded into the dark to give her an impression of his parting smile. It was really meant for her, who should have been in my place—the only blot on this last rapturous week was, he said, that she did not share it.

November 23

A CERTAIN amount of bad pain may be good for the moral character—I may as well think so, though I don't really believe in Purgatory. But pain prolonged is degeneration, not purgation. I am losing, coin by coin, the last of the treasure of patience I have been so carefully hoarding. It has reached the point that I want to remove the head of any one who merely walks boldly across my floor, thereby causing a faint vibration of my iron bed, which at once communicates itself to my hyper-responsive ankle. I have learned, among my pillows, an art of timid stillness that would give points to a mummy. At moments, as after dressings, it seems quite too perilous to take a long breath.

The reaction of the medical and nursing *entourage* to suffering whose prolongation they see no good reason for—as the infection is clearing up and the fractures presumably knitting—is interesting. Colonel Lambert meets it as a medical man, with specific remedies; he disapproves heartily of my wasting away on hospital chicken broth. Dr. M., who hates suffering, meets it as a surgeon by keeping out of my room save when he is led here for a dressing by one of the nurses who rule his days. Miss O. is very sympathetic that I can't enjoy the hothouse fruit provided by kind friends, but turns prickly when a spasm comes; irritated with herself, I suspect (she is so good and conscientious) because she has not been able to prevent it. A certain gentle, kinky-haired, red-cheeked English night nurse with a cockney accent is the only person who can really arrange my fracture pillows. I begin to understand the New Testament when, after two hours sometimes of weary waiting for her, I feel her healing touch.

She has charge of the babies who occasionally come into the world on the top floor and this morning, against all law and order, she brought one in to me, at the pallid and cynical hour of two. A Swedish baby about three weeks old which, when unrolled from its warm, sweet-smelling blankets, blinked wisely at the light. A miracle of a baby, complete in every detail! Not a bone missing!

What saves me is that I am, even in my worst hours, more concerned with life and its mysteries than with the dykes that fate has built to hem it in and hinder its flow. But sometimes I am aware what a vicarious version of life I am getting—all through other people's eyes. Even the baby was held up at a distance. I am impatient to touch life again, to feel it swirling hard against my own body.

Life took me at my word. I am still shaken from head to foot by the shock of immersion. Dr. M. (more regardful than Miss O. and I gave him credit for) appeared to announce my immediate departure to "Number One" to be X-rayed. Before I knew it the revolution was accomplished: a stretcher with several friendly privates to hoist it had invaded my domain from the garden, and I was lying in an ambulance with keen outdoor air—how rough to the nostrils—rushing in at the open end, and a blurred vision of Neuilly flowing along behind: comfortable, high, brick, bourgeois mansions draped, above their discreet gardens, in the flags of victory. The ambulance boy did his best for me—"I never went so slow before"—but the jolting was excruciating on these boulevards rutted so deeply by four years of ambulances. It took no more than one jolt to translate me again into *unanimisme.*

The sensation of being translated into the body of a soldier, and into the "system" in which he lives and moves and has his being was further borne out as follows: *(a)* Irksome delay at the door. *(b)* Hot altercation between ambulance boy and sergeant in charge. The former claims that this entrance will save the patient; the latter "knows his orders"—so we eventually jolt along to the other one. *(c)* Appearance on the steps, as the stretcher is taken out, of two or three pretty nurse's aides of our best New York families, who gather around (blankets envelop me, and a grey hood like a monk's cowl falls over my head), inquiring in tones whose imperious and patronizing ring make me squirm with indignity, who this poor dear boy is, etc. *(d)* Journey the whole length of the hospital on a jiggly stretcher-cart to an elevator that isn't running. Journey the whole distance back to another that goes up only two stories. Thereafter journey the same distance back again to a long flight of stairs up which I am carried at an angle of forty-five degrees to the X-ray room. *(e) Interim*—endless wait by the second elevator (man having his lunch) in a corridor full of French *femmes de service* who are carrying lunch-trays to the wards. Unimaginable clatter of dishes, chatter of ten thousand magpies. The new patient intrigues the magpies, especially the youngish specimens, and they close in two or three deep about the stretcher-cart, gazing at the drawn features under the cowl with tilted, frizzed heads and loving, pitying, languorous looks that stifle like a heavy perfume.

Suddenly one soft creature gives away the show: *"On dirait une femme*—you'd say it was a woman," she breathes.

"It *is* a woman!" I answer furiously.

The ranks simply melt!

The X-ray itself, a skilful doctor in charge, was the least part of the business. But by the time the process *a, b, c, d, e,* etc., had been gone through in reverse order, from the top floor on the boulevard Inkermann to the ground floor on the rue Chauveau, I was in a state of acute and agonized exhaustion. There promised to be another wait before I could be moved from the stretcher to the bed—nurses at lunch. But there I spoke up, in the manner of Queen Elizabeth or Amy Lowell, and demanded that the stretcher-boys put me *at once* into the flat, still, waiting bed. (They were only too ready to help, but Miss O. was fearfully shocked.) I then demanded, in the voice of Julius Caesar or Napoleon, a hypodermic. It came too, and quickly (pity I didn't discover earlier how thoroughly it pays to lose one's self-control) and with it a young French nurse with sweet ways and piquant looks, who reminded me of my old friend Annie Wood and who held my hand while the Red Cross nurse—who never holds my hand—we are far too reserved together—had some lunch.

The afternoon was haunted by solicitous faces disappearing into space, and by a queer, faint voice (not at all a royal voice) pleading for silence and solitude: "Please don't let them come in... draw the curtains closer... send them away... don't let any one take me out of bed..."

A pitiable figure of a *unanimiste* I make now.

November 25

FOR two days all I have asked of the universe was to stay forever immured from it. To see nothing, hear nothing, for myself. But this morning's newspapers have restored a healthy and instinctive exasperation at the substitute for firsthand observation offered by the printed word.

To-day the French are entering Strasbourg; yesterday it was the Americans entering Luxembourg; the day before, the French in Colmar; the day before that, King Albert in Brussels. And all this very true and profound emotion—for the return of the Belgian King to his capital is profoundly moving, and so, whether or not one has a doubt of its entire rightness, the return of the French to the lost provinces—is frozen and imprisoned in phrases of conventional patriotic fervor. And the events forthwith appear to have been invented as stunts—bread and circuses to amuse and placate the weary peoples. It seems ironic that the very instrument which did most to create the moral alliance against Germany has so far discredited its own influence that one now scents dishonesty even where it is not.

Take the Alsace-Lorraine question. During the war one's French liberal and radical friends admitted freely that the issue was not black-and-white. H. B. was the only liberal I can remember who insisted that it was a question of flat justice, restoration of stolen property. I wonder what his response would be to a passage from Arthur Young—the famous eighteenth-century English traveller—who, after a journey in 1789, represents the French as the original offenders against justice:

I found myself to all appearance in Germany.... Here not one person in a hundred has a word of French.... Looking at a map of

France and reading histories of Louis XIV never threw his conquest, or seizure, of Alsace into the light which travelling into it did: to cross a great range of mountains; to enter a level plain inhabited by a people totally distinct and different from France, with manners, language, ideas, prejudices, and habits all different, made an impression of the injustice and ambition of such conduct much more forcible than ever reading had done; so much more powerful are things than words.... Alsace is Germany, and the change great on descending the mountains.... The moment you are out of a large town, all in this country is German.

It was Rick who called my attention to these observations. Because they tallied with his own when he was driving an ambulance in Alsace in 1916. He has a charming story of a *vielle demoiselle* with whom he lived at Mollau, and her French flag hidden away for forty-four years of secret loyalty. But he says she was the only person of French speech and tradition in that town and is very dubious whether the return of the French will be welcomed by the majority. The two Alsatian sisters among the pupil nurses—admirably and distinguishedly of the French tradition—do much to reassure me. Of course one is sentimentally for France. Never did intellectual misgivings seem more ungracious. Dau-det's "La Derniere Classe" made so deep an impression on me at the age of thirteen that I was almost moved to tears, last year, in Alsace *reconquise,* when I saw one of the old schoolmasters of before 1870 teaching the guttural-mouthed children their lessons in French. Yes, sentiment has won the day—until one reads the sugary platitudes in the press.

I was mentally damning the whole tribe of journalists when in walked L. S. G.—delighted to agree with me, but frankly glad to be back *en civil* as one of them,—I must say it is a pleasure to see somebody not in uniform,—as correspondent of *The Survey* for the Conference. He has the real journalist's passion for nosing about the town, eating in odd places, standing on street corners and letting the winds of report blow through his ears, and then journeying to distant alleys to interview greasy individuals who prove report false. Jouhaux and Longuet and Merrheim are becoming his closest intimates. He brought me *La Bataille* which avoids all mention of

Strasbourg by featuring the peace programme of the French working-class as drawn up by the *Confederation Generale du Travail* in accord with Wilson's Fourteen Points. The degree to which Wilson is trusted by French labor makes one fearful... Witness even the advertisements on the back page. One *confrere* offers envelopes adorned with the portrait of the great citizen Wilson, President of the Republic of the United States... no more expensive than the ordinary envelope... all our readers should try this useful, practical, and economical way of honoring the illustrious friend of France."

Dr. M. burst in, in his uniform, with my X-ray pictures while L. S. G. was still here and found his worst suspicions of his patient's radicalism confirmed by the presence of a peculiarly disarming young man in a soft collar, with a Socialist newspaper in one hand and a volume of Chinese poetry in the other. This welcome visitor of the free and inquiring spirit always brings me some book or other, as well as all sorts of goodies—which is just what you might expect of a man who is married and a pacifist.

The doctor was very warm about the X-rays, beamed with such a boyish happiness that the fractures had knit, that I felt touched and reproached. But my left foot has dropped out of position and must be put into a plaster cast—with a hole large enough for dressings. Query suppressed by New England pride: how does the *blessed* feel when the foot is twisted back to a right angle with the leg? I shall know soon enough.

Meanwhile I nibble at Arthur Waley's versions of the ancient and sage Chinese, wondering dimly why they make me homesick for New York. I have it! They remind me of a picture I once saw at the British Museum—a Confucian sage, deep in meditation by a cataract on a high mountainside. And Herbert Croly, sunk in meditation as deep over his long cigar, with his glass of milk beside him and the sound of many disputatious voices in his ears, is, at the *New Republic* lunch-table, the very image of the Chinese sage. I had such a kind letter from Croly to-day. The *New Republic* lunch-table, for all its disconcerting qualities, is a place I'd like to be....

November 26

THE milestones in hospital lives are not very conspicuous, but I am aware of having reached one to-day. Indeed it lies, very white and heavy, in the bottom of my bed—a cast on my left leg.

My room is the first on the downstairs corridor, so my journey on the stretcher-cart to the examining-room, which is just to the right of the front door, was very brief. The point is that in spite of the bad results of the last journey, and in spite of the certainty of torture, I took it with anticipation—the anticipation of a new experience. And the glimpse I had of hospital geography gave me a sort of mental orientation with the outside world that I do not repudiate as I did last time, now that I am back in my bed. I don't even repudiate the two Y.M.C.A. men I saw engaged in patient absorption of the fifteen-cent magazines in the big reception-room that opens with much glass on the garden. I merely noted that the species had not been changed by the Armistice. Unmistakable in flavor as a Russian novel, or Italian spaghetti.

Dr. M. was in great spirits, and for once I was well enough to like the jokes and the bustle. He kept his clever Spanish assistant—who looks like a soubrette; also as if she would knife a rival in the back with pleasure—very busy getting things ready, while the hearty English pupil nurse was despatched to fetch me " forty drops." The doctor has a high regard for cognac. In fact he administered forty drops before as well as after the ordeal. I was, therefore, sufficiently braced to take in the odd expression on his face as he manipulated my poor foot (so he always refers to it). He looked like a little boy with his hand in a Christmas stocking, very uncertain of the value of the object he was going to fish out of the depths. Well, Dr. M. pulled out, not a mandarin orange, but a real present from Santa Claus. The ankle joint worked! Excruciatingly, but actually. Whereupon he began to quote Falstaff so loud and joyously that I stifled my groans in sheer amazement. For my surgeon had not struck me as a Shakespearian personage. When the cast was safely on, the foot self-respectingly erect inside, and a large hole cut over the wound, he assured me, with his nicest smile (which I had never seen before) that "if God is good"—Miss O. greatly distressed by his blasphemy—I should have a useful leg yet.

"Swing it around your head any time you like, now," he called after me as they trundled me off.

A fear that I haven't dared express, even to myself, has by the movement of that joint been hauled out of the subconscious. Then there is this new light on Dr. M., as somebody who might become friendly and conversable during convalescence. Thus do I make terms, to-night, with my aching milestone.

November 27

A WONDERFUL visitor this morning: Dr. Simon Flexner, who has been in France a few weeks on a Red Cross mission, and learned by chance of my accident and whereabouts. I had never seen him in uniform. It admirably suits his bald, eagle-like head, his profile of a Roman senator.

By some mistake he had been kept waiting in the reception-room, and had an autocratic taxi-driver, who allowed him just twenty minutes at the hospital, on his conscience. (What a nose the fellows have for newly arrived Americans. It takes an old Parisian like me to face them down.) But every second he stole from the autocrat was infinitely precious to me. After so much of comradely and egotistic youth, so much of mere kindly war-acquaintance in the shape of visitors, the sight of this sagacious and affectionate older friend made something stir in the depths of me. He did not pretend that I was a slightly ailing hostess in a salon to be addressed on general topics with crossed legs. He drew a chair beside me and took my hand, and it seemed that every bad hour in six poignant weeks was compensated by the sympathy and keen understanding in his eyes.

He realized that he was making me homesick—for no amount of bluff can prevent him from knowing exactly how one feels—and left me a few consoling pictures to keep by me: pictures of a country where white-clad scientists still stood by laboratory tables, disturbed by no more ominous rumblings than those of elevated trains; where in green-embowered academic halls the faces of young girls were still ravished by the dim enchantments of the Faery Queen.... He brought me back to France with a diverting account of his unexpected celebration of Armistice night at a French hospital in the war zone where he and Dr. Lambert had had to ask shelter—and were more than warmly welcomed for the sake of poliomyelitis. Of course he extracted my whole story—that is one of his subtlest arts. And then, of course, he went. Wisdom tarries with us such a little, little while. Then we fall back into the depths of our own insufficiency—which we try to make as gallant as we can, so that wisdom may not be sorry it took a look at us.

November 28

TEN A.M. Enter Dr. M., hurried and professional, his white *chemise* flapping against his military boots, followed by the usual trail of cigarette smoke and Miss G., carrying a strange implement which turns out to be a plaster-cutter.

"I'm going to cut down your cast well below the knee, my child."

Blessed (aggrieved): "Just as it gets comfortable."

"To make it more comfortable. There! Now try to bend your knee. You see, Colonel?"—to Miss G.—"Stiff as a ramrod. Now, you've got to bend it every day, no matter how it hurts. If not, the Colonel and I shall anaesthetize you and do it forcibly. By the time that great and good man President Wilson (whom I swear I disown, even if I *am* a Southerner) arrives to *ennuyer* M. Clemenceau, I expect you to be able to rest your chin on it."

Exit *en coup de vent,* leaving Miss O. and me to the new morning occupation of knee-bending.

At eleven comes Colonel Lambert with his blend of the Rooseveltian and Mephistophelian—square, burly shoulders that deny the implications of his dark, pointed beard and snapping brown eyes. He carries a large bunch of Parma violets, hoping in their delicious perfume to disguise the bitter flavor of his news: he has his orders and is sailing in December. The words are scarcely out before R. M. follows him in, looking grave under her Red Cross hat because she has the same news to tell: she is going home for Christmas. My two chief Paris props knocked out from under me at the same time!

It does make me feel light-headed for a moment. Not only that they have been so perfect in kindness, kept such a constant, responsible eye upon me ever since I drove up to the F. etc. in that midnight ambulance. What hits me harder, I believe, is the idea that the American Red Cross can run without these two high authorities; for that means that *the war is over*—psychologically. Physically, it has been over for some sixteen days. But in fact its images and symbols have, if my head and the heads of my visitors are any indication, continued completely to preoccupy us.

Now the readjustment has come. The clock of destiny is about to strike the hour that will banish from the Paris stage the servitors of war. The peace-makers, waiting impatiently for the signal to take their places, will make no bones of turning the war-workers into the streets (a new hotel requisitioned every day—the bumptiousness of them, after we have saved Paris, say the war-workers.) Far better to go, as these two perspicacious people are doing, before the era with which they have been so deeply associated ends, and the character of Paris changes. I long to go, too. Considering the intensity of my own connection with the war period it is a strange fate that will keep me skewered to a bed on the periphery of the Peace Conference while, one by one, my war-time friends are off to the U.S.A.

The era of the war and of the Hotel de France et Choiseul. Never again shall we all sit in that courtyard under a glass roof pierced by shrapnel, drinking caustic coffee served by the lugubrious Charles and sugared from our personal stores, while the stars prick patterns in the deep purple of the sky, and in a yellow window square a typewriter begins to tap. Tap-tap-tap: come-in-to-work. No, another ten minutes. There'll be a raid by that time. Besides, Colonel Lambert is reporting some "inside" gossip from G.H.Q. Mr. Ford has details about the devastated regions. Mrs. Ford and Mrs. Lambert are discussing the latest freaks in behavior in women war-workers. One of the Rockefeller doctors draws up a chair to tell how the sub-prefect of a certain department took him fishing for shrimps—it is done with beefsteak—in the interests of tuberculosis. And Gertrude pauses long enough in a dash from the street, where she has been picking up a lost private and finding him a night's lodging, to the room where six Y.M.C.A. workers with grievances have been champing for several solid hours to relate an anecdote of a submarined negro stevedore:

"Ah tell you, miss, all ah asks of dis 'yere war is that ah shall be a *suhvivah."*...

The F. etc. without the Lamberts. Inconceivable! They should, on their departure, be presented with a set of "souvenirs": a square of prehistoric red carpet; a bronze and gold Empire clock under a glass case; and *(specialite de la maison, emu de M. le proprietaire)* a dozen bottles of that ineffable and heady golden wine of Touraine.

Evening

THE pain again. I feel as if my left leg were being squeezed in one of the iron boots the Inquisition invented for purposes of torture.

I wish Madame F. T. hadn't come on a day of pain, a day of *souvenirs* and departures. Yet perhaps that was the right time, for her heart and mind are still sore with war and grief. Her mother, who was very ill during my last long stay with her in the country, died just after my accident.

She sat down quietly beside me in the darkened room. But there is something nobly unresigned in this French woman, who carries her head with a poise that few women achieve—the more bonds that life puts upon her, the more she constrains herself to resignation and quietude, the blacker the veil which drapes that head, the more unquiet the essence of the spirit, the more gorgeous the gleam of the red hair and white skin through the veil. I could lie here forever and look at her.

Her first words take me straight back to November 11th.

"Ah, *there amie,* you are fortunate not to have seen Paris on the day of the Armistice—you who love Paris. It was dreadful! What disillusion in this poor, petty human nature which reacts so basely from its fine emotions! How can you Protestants put the confidence you do in the human will? It has no strength at all when the mysterious force of life reasserts itself."

I saw her spurning the streets, scorching the pageantry and the easy *détente* with those fierce, violet eyes.

"Think what the war has been to my family alone. One of the least afflicted."

Your family! I do think of it constantly, and with gratitude, as I lie here. In its two perfect settings. In the old house on the *quaff* with the poplars along the Seine crinkling their leaves under the windows—the house where two broad streams of French tradition, Catholic and Protestant, literary and artistic, mingle so happily. In the little, half-timbered country house next your mother's above the valley near Versailles where you have welcomed me to a still more intimate and gracious rusticity. A family always, in spite of its simplicity of heart, in spite of its hospitality to all sorts and conditions of men and opinions *("chez moi,"* you once said to me, *"c'est tout ce qu'il y a de plus salade")* looking down on the world with the remoteness of achieved perfection. Always bathed in the most golden light of France—until the war turned the whole French sky lurid.

I think especially of a night at the end of May, six months ago, when you and I sat up far into the small hours. We are in your husband's study which seems, even by day, detached from the material universe. A spot of perfect peace and isolation such as writers dream, but never possess out of France: opening with a great window and suspended, as by a mysterious cord let down from the sky, above your deep, somnolent vale. To-night the valley is dark; only a gleam from the moon on the roof of an old château, the spire of the village church. Only one earthly light, the yellow eye of the *gare*.

But into the room flows a strong, intermittent pulsation: the guns of the front. Nearer, more insistent every hour. And so you are packing a few things. Your beautiful household linen. Your husband's notebooks. Now and then you pause in your investigation of one of his cupboards to show me your daughter's first sketch-book (that certainly must go in. The child had an extraordinary gift for caricature). The last birthday gift of your younger brother, killed in early September, 1914, before his poor little wife had even had a letter from him, several months before the birth of his child. If only that cuckoo would stop! Waked, perhaps, by the guns, he is mocking and calling in the dark tops of your ancient trees. And the scent of roses and heliotrope floating on puffs of warm wind.

Standing at the window I hear a new sound against the reverberation of cannon: a rumbling, a squeak of brakes, a shrill whistle; a troop train. Slowly it winds its caterpillar way up the dreaming valley, breaking the white mist with a heavier column of white smoke.

"How many times in the last four years," you say, from your knees on the floor, "my second brother has travelled through our valley with his big guns on a train like that, on his way to a new sector—just seeing the tops of our roof and my mother's. Sometimes he manages to send up a line by the *chef de gare.*"

(I lunched with them both on the *quaff* in 1912, I remember, when he was a successful young novelist and a delicate *precieux* instead of an artillery officer).

The number of images and thoughts that can flash through one's head in two minutes.

"F. is in Alsace, you know," goes on my visitor. "He is sending you a letter about it. It's been a very great emotional experience, a sort of compensation for all his disintegrating war service of the rear."

So your husband, my black-bearded friend, comes to join us. I see him wandering like a lost soul in his Paris library on one of his leaves, seeking—for his generous, curious intelligence must always be seeking—the significance of Wilson. Discussing at lunch the implications of the American intervention. But the sort of lucid searching and fine-spun deducing to which his mind is accustomed is bustled and deadened by the material conditions in which it must work, and still more by preoccupation with the destiny of France. To him the personal cost of the war is, I believe, a very subtle cost in intellectual freedom.

Your boy, coming in from his *lycee* to take his place at the lunch-table—absurdly like his father—complains of a loss in intellectual stimulus. All his teachers are so weary, and so dull, and so old. The young, vital ones are dead or fighting.

Your daughter has no complaints to make as she starts out for her war-work, with her wavy, willowy gait. (She is more than half your age—for you were married at seventeen—and has a bloom like a peach, and lips red as *midinettes* cannot make them with all the rouge of the *Galeries*. Her dress has a *nuance* of the more romantic era of those two grandmothers who have been, perhaps, her closest friends.) She loves to nurse refugee babies, and do up bundles for prisoners. She loves to write letters. (Yes, I have looked up and seen her, many a time, bending her small, modelled head, on its slim neck, over her writing-table in the window where she sits like an enchanted princess under the tree-tops.) It is you who sigh that she doesn't know what she is missing; that the years from sixteen to twenty are normally the only gay and irresponsible ones in a French girl's life. She has spent those years in such anxious and elderly society! Never to meet a young man save on a leave, with the doom of death ahead...

"If you knew, *ma chere,* the recalcitrant thoughts I have dug into my carrot patch."

I do know, for I have watched you digging—with fury and determination. Gardening has been the chief of your war-work—with the adoption into your family of some young refugees. You have a native gift with peasant boys, as well with carrots and bees and goats. Yet only an aristocrat can wear *sabots* as you do. And shall I ever forget the day of rich September, when, in a moment of joy, standing in the midst of the war-time flock you had settled in your rose garden, you suddenly, laughing, seized your old ram by the beard and drew him prancing like Capricorn on an antique coin across the terrace, while the sun burnished your copper hair and the young kids skipped about you?

Can that be only two months ago? The face under the black veil is tragic. She is preparing to go; regretting that she lives so far, asking what books and food she can send me. And she has a last word:

"Whenever, during these four years, I took a train I used to wish I might go on travelling, on and on, never stopping till the nightmare was over. But now it is over I have no sense of reaching a goal. Wherever one looks, blackness and devastation.. No doubt the separation has been hard for American wives and mothers—but how brief! And your men go back to an-untouched country. Forgive me," she added, squeezing my hand. "I am violent and passionate. At least I used to be passionate. I am still violent. And I revolt."

She is gone, and I think of my morning visitors. It is true that six months from now Dr. Lambert will be so plunged in his recovered practice that his two years and a half of war-time Paris will seem a dream. R. M. will again be using the resources that have so finely served the Red

Cross in New York civic activities. And New York won't look or feel very different. But the house on the *quai*—though no bomb pierced the roof—and the house over the valley—though the linen and the *souvenirs d'enfance* are back in their cupboards—will be changed. The golden light that bathed them and gave your spirits their special ease and limpidity before 1914 has vanished.

November 29

THANKS to my friends, who have thrown a mirage of their diverse impressions on my grey wall, I have "seen" the Armistice celebrated in Paris and at the front. And now, on top of Madame T.'s visit, to the sound of the salutes that announce King George's arrival in Paris, comes the promised letter from F. T. Such a number of delicately written sheets! I fall on them avidly, for his observations are sure not to be dictated in advance by Nationalism or *Revanche* or any other cult.

"I should be ashamed of my long silence," he begins, "if one of the greatest shocks of my life were not its excuse. Why were you not there, *there mademoiselle? I* shall not try to turn your thoughts away from the sights you have missed.

"I saw Metz first. I was one of the first to enter, carrying the first French newspapers, which I distributed for more than three hours to the crowd; and I assure you it was moving, the old men, the old women, the young men, the children, the old people especially, coming out of all the doors with hands outstretched for these first papers in their language—forbidden for four years. Metz is nevertheless the city where our reception was the least vigorous, the least violently enthusiastic. It is a city with no industrial life, which has always lived by its garrison and its officials. None has been more deformed by subjection. Yet I did not think that experience could be surpassed. I was suspicious of the cities of German speech. My poor reason had given me no inkling of what patriotism without a linguistic foundation could be.

"After that I saw Thionville, a small city in Lorraine where the French tongue still predominates. But all through the villages of the region it was German that was spoken. Ah, Thionville! That exquisite morning at the gate of the old town, all the bells ringing and behind and about me the notables who had got out their silk hats—one wore his ancient uniform; and opposite me, on the other side of the road where the troops were to march past, the villagers, packed in close together, led by their *cures;* and behind the *cures* the young girls in costume what youth, what freshness!—wearing on their shoulders exquisite shawls which had just been taken out of old *armoires;* beautified, softened by a hundred years in lavender.

"'*Mesdemoiselles,* what pretty shawls! Where do they come from?'

"'Our grandmothers!' replied the young things proudly.

"Finally, after twenty minutes of waiting, the bugles, the drums, the troops—these troops so handsome and so grave, these battalions of survivors, these proven faces, happy and astonished to be so....

"If you had seen the emotion of the old, the happiness of the young girls, who saw at last these soldiers of whom their grandmothers used to talk, these soldiers to whom so many of their brothers had fled soldiers of *theirs, their* soldiers, you would have understood, as never before, what an ancient, instinctive, profoundly natural and real thing the *patrie* is. And if you had seen their half-open lips, their fixed eyes, their arms and hands raised and stretched out toward the men—that beautiful antique gesture of acclamation which I had seen so awkwardly and badly suggested by the actors of the Theatre Francais, discovered and repeated by the girls of Lorraine! And the troops kept on passing; infantry and cavalry, heavy and light artillery, and always the bells, the sun, the cries, and the ecstasy—the same still, sustained note of the most ancient human enthusiasm—the most ancient and the youngest.

"Shall I tell you about Strasbourg? I have never been able to describe it. It is one of the most beautiful cities in Europe. Its cathedral is inferior to none. The sharp, chiselled mass, all in red sandstone, colored as by an eternal dawn, rises above a narrow square. No promenade of ancient France is pleasanter than its Broglie. No square of the eighteenth or nineteenth century, of revolutionary France, has more grandeur than the place Kléber. It is a very mysterious mediaeval city, a very magnificent royal city, a very thriving modern city. Throw into it a vehement people, a victorious army, hundreds of enchanted young girls wearing their imposing costume—there is a setting!

"Well, if you please, imagine now, evoke if you can an emotion so strong that all this exterior is, as it were, crushed, extinguished. I have seen a summer in Calabria. There are two or three hours in the afternoon when the blue sea, the marble sands, seem to be melted, dissolved in the might of the sun. At Strasbourg it was the same: the visible scene was, as it were, absorbed by the might of the emotions, by their radiance.

"The visible scene I did not neglect, you may be sure. I am a fairly experienced observer and I traversed Strasbourg from end to end, sometimes ahead of the band which preceded Petain, sometimes behind it, beside Petain's carriage. Following the edges of the massed crowd, walking ahead of the music, with the brasses bellowing in the back of my neck, and flowers showering about me, I watched the faces which bent at our approach like spears of grain; these faces expressed ecstasy, and I don't know how many hundreds of ecstasies thus touched and pierced me in my rapid walk.

"Looking at the faces, picking up the flowers, I did not give myself up to the mysticism of emotion; I tried to understand what was going on about me. And I discerned in this mighty and apparently single wave which bathed me different sorts of waves—I am going to tell you what they were.

"I modestly begin with the one that to me as a Frenchman is the least touching, the least flattering; that joyous physical relaxation and relief which peace has produced everywhere. I have just read a German description of the entry of the troops into Berlin. The facts are strangely like those that I noted in Strasbourg. The horror is ended. The men are coming back: joy of the young girls, a simple joy: they are going to dance.

Remember that not one of these young girls who are eighteen in Europe to-day has ever danced. At Strasbourg they were mad as every girl is at the end of her first cotillion, and their madness spread contagiously through their whole city.

"Secondly, there was *la Patrie*. I do not say France; I say *la Patrie*. I persevere in my modesty. There was *la Patrie,* distinct from France, pure and undifferentiated. This Alsatian people has been living for fifty years in a foreign frame. There has been joy in its homes, but in the market-place nothing—a desert and a wilderness. Worse still, a foreign parade, a parody of what no longer existed. I heard in the Strasbourg crowd a remark that was like a shaft of light. A woman said, as she watched our soldiers, *her* soldiers passing by, in the voice of a person coming out of a dream:

'Do you remember? When it was the *others* how little it meant to us!'

"'How little it meant'—that was a penetrating word. Not 'how it hurt'—no, Alsace was used to it, used to a sort of lack, a diminishing, a flatness. And suddenly, like a transformation-scene at the end of a long play, the German sinks out of sight, steals off with his effects tied up in a handkerchief. And here come the trumpets and drums and the army, the real one, this time, of which the grandmothers talked..

"The first Frenchman who entered Strasbourg did not come from France, but from Germany. He was a prisoner of war, the first to be set free. He crossed the bridge and walked straight toward the town. They ran out to meet him; they tried to shake hands with him. Red trousers! He was still wearing an old pair of red trousers. His knapsack was seized by the women. He did not understand what it was all about.

"'You're mistaken,' he said; 'I'm a prisoner.'

"'You're a Frenchman!' they cried. And a crowd followed him as he entered the town, leading him from one place to another, giving him cigars and sweets.

"'Ma foi,' he said, I don't mind if I do..

"A Frenchman: I must get there at last, and be done with modesty. There is, no doubt, in France something delicate and generous which calls out love. 'We are so glad to see you again,' said an Alsatian as he led me into his house; 'France has always been so good to us.' That, I think, is a truly Alsatian remark which expresses the difference that Alsace has always felt between herself and France, and at the same time the joy she has always had in feeling united to France. This marriage, remembered after fifty years, seems to have been not only good but delicious, one of those successes that La Rochefoucauld would declare impossible. The French domination has left only memories of happiness, prosperity, glory.

"I interrupt myself: it's true that the French domination has left no bad memories. But has it left memories? The Alsatian I have just quoted was a man of years and learning. But in those young heads that I took in, one by one, as I crossed Strasbourg, those happy young heads, what can the name of France evoke? Say in a girl of eighteen, the age of my daughter. Her two grandmothers are seventy years old. Traditions are handed on very well from a grandmother to her grandchildren. But that depends on the social class. Much of France is preserved in the bourgeoisie. But in the people, among the peasants? Old wives' grumblings: 'In the days of the French it was better.... The Germans are brutes.... The French aren't like the Germans... Every Alsatian knew that, and what a recommendation for us! But it's a rather negative piece of information. And remember always the difference of language: one powerful tie is completely lacking.

“What, then, is France, this country with an unknown tongue for these peasant girls? A face of which the features are growing dim, or altogether lacking. And yet the face is there. France is a country for which one has suffered much. For fifty years much; for the last four years very, very much. Her language, pleasant to hear, obstinately preserved by two or three families in every village, is forbidden. Whoever is caught saying a word is punished with fine or imprisonment. There is more. France is the country toward which thirty thousand young men fled to enlist as soldiers the first day of the war. Thirty thousand departures. Thirty thousand tragedies. Thirty thousand young men fighting of whom there is no news. Thirty thousand families who stay behind and are persecuted by Germany. And now the families are beginning to learn what has become of the young men, the young men what has become of the families. How many meetings and what pathos.... And all this pathos comes from France, the unknown *Patrie* which must be very beautiful because so much courage is spent for her and so many tears shed.

“I was waiting the entry of the troops at the Shirmeck Gate, and suddenly I saw, among the costumed groups, two young girls wearing light-colored flowered ribbons on their heads, instead of the usual black bows. I asked my nearest neighbor whether there were villages where light ribbons were worn. She answered: ‘No, we wear black ribbons since the other war since we stopped being French. Now that we are no longer in mourning, the flowers are coming back.’

“Fine elements for a legend? Yes, they abound. They will one day form one of the most beautiful episodes in history. Possibly the classic instance of Fidelity, as Jeanne d’Arc created, in the fifteenth century, the classic instance of *Salut*. Here is another fragment:

“The war brought France into Alsace; the army stayed on the border, but the aviators flew over the country. Alsace listened as they passed—listened and was not afraid. The Germans ran to hide in their cellars. They were afraid. They had to be afraid; they could not admit that Mulhouse, Colmar, and Strasbourg were not their towns, towns threatened by French bombers. But the Alsatians laughed and said: 'France is sparing us the war.' And it was true. This rich Alsace, this gage of war, this greatly desired captive, has remained four long years between the countries that were quarrelling over her, and the war has scarcely touched her.

"And France has done more: to spare Alsace she has sacrificed some of her finest provinces. Metz, Strasbourg, Colmar, Mulhouse, are untouched. But Verdun, Rheims, Soissons, Arras, are destroyed. Alsace knows it, knows it and is moved by it. Alsace knows, too, the human cost of her return: more than fifteen hundred thousand lives, as many dead as there are living in Alsace and Lorraine. For every living soul in Alsace a man in France and of France has fallen....This takes us deep into the legend.

"Let us return to reality. What is France, the real France for this Alsatian people which is acclaiming her? Visibly and palpably it is an army: an army with a supple step which does not hammer the soil as the other did. Officers whose looks do not insult as the others did. One man embodies France for the people of Strasbourg: General Gouraud. He has led the first troops in, he commands the town. A magnificent presence: a long face, elegant, military, ascetic. The face of a gentleman, a priest, a soldier. One sleeve drops: an arm is missing. When he walks he is unsteady: he has an injured hip. But these bodily weaknesses enhance the man, increase his radiance. I hear the cry:

"*Vive* Gouraud!'

"The success of the army is prodigious. Officers and soldiers both are endowed with all the virtues. What is more extraordinary, I believe that they have them. The long trial of the trenches has not made them brutal; rather, more patient, more experienced, more delicate. How little are they drunkards, how little *poilus!* I see them full of attentions, charming with these young girls in beautiful costumes, these fairy shepherdesses who throw themselves into their arms, murmuring French words a little awkwardly. The grandmothers then spoke true; the French are as kind as they are valiant, and as sensitive as they are gallant. What is more, these charming French are also the strong. The Empire, the monstrous Empire, is no more; it has fallen, and in its fall it has broken. And now comes back France the light, the well-beloved, and miraculously the really strong, since it is she who has conquered.

"The morning after the day when Petain entered Strasbourg, thanksgiving services were held in the churches. The cathedral is Alsace itself, the parish of this province. The interior, with its height, its elegance, its robustness, the mystery of its transepts and distant chapels, are brightened by the naïve and gay colors of the flags fastened to the pillars of the nave. The people are standing, eager, silent. The flags of the Corporations come in and pass by. The French officers file in and mount to the altar. They occupy the right of the choir, the priests the left. In the middle, two young girls dressed in the striking fete-day costume of Catholic Alsace: gold head-dress with bright red ribbons framing a long flag of white silk. An old priest mounts to the pulpit and speaks:

'God be praised: France, here thou art. For fifty years we have dwelt in hope of thee, and here thou art.... A few years ago one of our old friends died in this city. He had hoped all his life, and the moment had come for him to renounce earthly hopes. He gathered his children about him: "My children, I shan't see the French. But you'll see them, and when they are here you must come to my grave and call very loud: `Father, here are the French!' " Let us shout it to our dead: "Fathers, mothers, the French are here!" And let us promise them to love France as they themselves did; more, if possible, for we know all she has just sacrificed for us.'

"Te Deum laudamus—I hear the sacred chant that follows as a tragic marriage hymn. The history of Alsace has always appeared to me in the form of a love story. Alsace is a woman torn from the man she loved, slowly re-creating for herself a resigned calm that she can call happiness, and that will perhaps become so.... The man comes back, he alone counts, she is in his arms.... But the future? May they be happy, may they be happy! The mystic bell has rung; the officers kneel, I kneel, too, and when I arise and open my eyes I see the two serious young girls with head-dresses of shining red and gold kneeling at my feet on the tiled floor. May they be happy, may they be happy!"

***

Miss O. turns the *Saturday Evening Post* with a rustle, and suddenly these radiant, living scenes are gone. Clean vanished away. Nothing left of them but some handfuls of paper covered with decorative hieroglyphics, scattered over the bed.

The bed. I recognize it with surprise. Slowly I make the tour of my room. White *armoire a glace*. White mantel with rows of books. White writing table. French window. White *chaise longue*. White washstand. White chair. White nurse. Grey-white door. Bed—hard and white, with bars and rivets of pain. Everything pale and purged.

The white nurse shivers as she reads. The atmosphere is chill, and the grey-white French winter daylight that comes through the door. The sun has gone into permanent hibernation, and I can't believe those gaunt trees ever had golden leaves.

By shutting my eyes I recapture the illusion, though. Happy streets of Strasbourg. Luminous cathedral—" In France there is something delicate and generous that calls out love." How blest I am to have French friends with exquisite perceptions, who take such exquisite pains to make me see....

Yet nobody's else spectacles really fit. F. T. is a liberal and an intellectual, but (I tell myself) he can't help approaching the Alsatian affair as an *affaire de coeur*. What Frenchman can—or should? As Pascal finely said, *le coeur a ses raisons que la raison ne connait pas*. His delicious picture leaves out every element that the heart cannot accept unchallenged. It no more deals with reason—for all his effort to escape from the "mysticism of emotion "—than, in another field, New-man's "Apologia."

Moreover, the scenes he describes are bathed—he would admit it himself—in a special, enhancing light, like the light after sunset in which people stand out in very sharp outline, yet a little transfigured. I am beginning to mistrust that light which is, I am surer and surer, the reflection cast by the battle-fields. Not only Alsace and France, but England and France, France and America, have, during these war years, seen each other in its flush. So long as millions of men were thirsting and bleeding and dying together, the ardor of their sacrifice glorified all relations behind the lines.

I fear for us all—the fear grows into a horror 1 during the still sleepless and interminable nights—a reaction from this exalted *entente.* Especially for the two nations I love best. American stock in France has been abnormally high; and the French cause had been steadily romanticized by America. That was unfair, for the French themselves had no sense, during the war, of being supermen. They went about their job of soldiering as they used to do that of peasant, professor, workman. Their daily effort was to minimize their pain, conceal their wounds under a twisted smile. (I remember a certain aristocrat, directing us to the ruins of his ancestral *chateau* in the Somme, which the Germans had blown up with dynamite: "*Vous allez rigoler!")* Not supermen, but men and *ga-lantes gens* who in blood and territory bore the brunt of the war.

We must not forget that at the Peace Conference. But the inspired French press should stop reminding us. The psychological effect is disastrous, after the nation's fine reticence. I don't believe the most sensitive Frenchman—for even he has a certain hard-headedness realizes how it jars on the softly sentimental American when the Quai d'Orsay turns *Madame la patronise,* and presents the bill. It is the tone of the *Echo de Paris* that one minds, more than the bill. Only the Socialist papers protest, imploring that Wilson make good the loss and the idealist hope of the war.

F. T.'s fearful *"qu'ils soient heureux"* rings in my ears to-night. I repeat, till I am hypnotized into apathy, *"qu'ils soient heureux, qu'ils soient heureux.."*

November 30

RICK is gone, definitely so far as Neuilly is concerned, and the last door that remained ajar on the war is closed.

He came out for his good-bye visit by devious routes—to avoid King George, who is still royally processing—bringing a bunch of red roses, which he laid bashfully on the bed. The last time he appeared, with Tom, he had one foot in the empyrean. To-day he was wistful and depressed—thoughts of Brest and Paris endings. He is a Meredithian young man, self-absorbed at either end of the temperamental scale, whether headed for the zenith or the central abyss.

Talk disjointed as usual. He'd give his bottom dollar (very gloomily) to stay and see the troops march under the Arc de Triomphe. Tom (cheering up to a grin) pitched into him for saying that. Told him the end of the war ought to mean more to him than a cheap celebration.... Well, of course. But men vary.

"They say war is inhuman. I never knew what brotherhood was before. Never really got outside my class. War is human. It's more than that—it deifies human relations!"

What conviction in his voice and his long jaw. Every word gloriously true for his own experience. Thank God there are many other men, especially in the A.E.F., for whom war has been personally a heightening of power and a broadening of sympathy. But how would Rick feel if he had lost a leg and with it that abounding vitality? If he had had three or four years at the front? Would his emotions have swung the circle till he found himself with Sassoon and the young Englishmen who have survived to complete disillusion and a burning creed of anti-war?

Before he went we drank Dr. M.'s pint bottle of champagne, the one that arrived too late to celebrate the Armistice. Miss O. had kept it secreted all this while and served it warm (oh, North Dakota!) in a tumbler and a medicine glass. But Rick gulped the vapid beverage down, bringing out with some difficulty that his sister and I were the " best friends he had in the world." (He is going back to her safe. Safe! It *is* a miracle. My trust and my charge are over.)

The poor fellow is more and more tormented by the prowling and rapacious spectres of future literary projects. He doesn't yet know whether he is going to swallow them or they him. I remember too well how I felt at a similar age and moment. The writing "disposition" is a queer mixture of self-confidence and self-distrust—and America is well calculated to quash the confidence. Here in France, where there is group support for authors, and very general belief besides in the worth of creative work *versus* money-getting, a young writer with a real gift can rise on his wings straight and unafraid. With us such a man gets no cheers from the bystanders as he prepares to leave the ground. On the contrary, to his secret doubts is added the open scepticism of the community. Rick will find that when he returns....

Yet one dares to urge him to be a writer? Well, America needs him. These young men who have survived their great adventure have a very special contribution to make, and I wish they were all endowed in the cause of literature. For they are experienced, yet fresh in energy. Genuinely democrats, yet men of the world in the widest sense. They have shared with the least articulate of their countrymen primitive emotions that identify them forever with the substrata of their native land, yet Europe too has adopted them as she never really adopted American aliens before. They have worn her colors, served her without slavishness, offered their blood in transfusion for her veins. A magnificent foundation to build on, especially when is added a fierce and hungry need to do something big enough to match the war and its masculinity. Why should not the result be a new and great era in American letters? Are these wounded fancies?

All I can do for Rick is to believe that his wings will uphold him. The faith that he can't come to grief in any flight he adventures has ever been the core of our understanding. *Bonne chance!*

So many things to do in the world, and here am I passively contemplating this spotless hospital ceiling with a mind all tangled up in the cobwebby problems of American literature and nobody to talk to but a good girl (good as gold, and ever so good to me) whose favorite author is Gene Stratton Porter.

The visitor I should like to-night is B. B. It is hard to realize that our literary conversations will remain forever unfinished. He was just a few years too old for the war—in the thirties instead of the twenties—but it might not have mattered if he could have got into the army. The Red Cross job he took as substitute, in a high crusading spirit, left him morally unfertilized. So even if he had lived there would, perhaps, have been no literary harvest. Yet—who knows? Frustration brings forth its own harvest in its own way. He might at forty have written those stories.

In France B. B. would certainly have been a novelist or a *nouvelliste*. In England perhaps an essayist or a bookish Oxford don. In America he had resigned himself to journalism as a solution for the struggle for existence. No, not resigned himself, though he certainly preferred it to cheap literature. It never satisfied him, for he was temperamentally a person who creates something out of his own substance instead of recording fact from without, and the nostalgia of the unwritten masterpiece never left him. There was a dinner one rainy Paris night when the smouldering thoughts and regrets came out over some very superior *hors d'oeuvres*—pointed by the blandly patronizing attitude of the bankers at the head of the Red Cross to assistants who wielded the pen. The bankers were typical to him of the rulers of America, they loomed till they obscured the sun and the stars, and it seemed just not worth while, that night, to be scribbling in their shadow.

Yet it was (whether the bankers knew it or not) B. B. who put the work of the A.R.C. in France "on the map." We that had the run of his office will not forget its charmed atmosphere, the lightsome seriousness of which every stenographer partook, every one an ardent ally in interpretation. I see him getting up from his desk in his ill-fitting khaki—which exactly matched his skin and was treated as disregardfully as the tweeds which must have been his natural garb—his jerky, hesitating word, his eager, awkward gesture, suddenly transformed by that warm beam of a smile which concealed so many fine discriminations. He was as ready to welcome the French journalist as the American and as easily inspired his confidence. No one less supersensitive and humorous could have kept the Franco-American balance so level.

Discrimination again fostered his genius for friendship, an art into which he put all the grace he had been cheated of in literature. It was as if he decided that here at least he was sure of accomplishing something creative and individual. He gave himself so freely—for every friend, especially the humblest—to all the precious, old-fashioned courtesies and shades of gentle attention no modern man has time for—that he would not have had time for himself, perhaps, if those stories had been written. How touched he was by the farewell dinner organized by the Gannetts in Montmartre (place du Tertre, of course, scene of so many war dinners that went to the bottom of things), where we sang him out of countenance in our glasses of *yin gris* while the sallow, long-haired poets looked on from the other tables—unamazed. It takes a great deal to amaze a Montmartre poet, and B. B. would have made a very good French Bohemian himself, if his hair and his hats and his revolts had been given half a chance to grow—if he hadn't been a gentleman of the old Anglo-Saxon school after all!

But he was also, with mental reservations, a very good New Yorker. He wrote me after he got home how the town looked from the window of the Lafayette.... He would have bound New York and Paris together, in the years to come, for those with a stock of common memories. None of us can face not finding him there. Gone forever from our shores. Borne away on a great tide to an unknown land that may fit better into his secret valuations, his proud repressions and reserves, his obstinately subtle and tender scheme of things.

Sometimes it comes to me as a new and startling idea—yet I suppose it is one of the oldest in the universe—that the friends who have vanished during the smoke of battle, like young Stewart and B. B., are the ones who in the far future will remain most vividly alive for me. Symbols of this era, unchanged, in high relief like the figures on the Grecian Urn, while the " survivors "—Rick and Tom and the rest—will transform themselves into everyday citizens, gradually losing their identity with the Great War, drifting away into unknown paths....

***

"We are no other than a moving row

Of Magic Shadow-shapes that come and go."

Back and forth they move. Brooding, pleading, phantasms of this old, recurrent night-mood. A *poilu's* face, white and cavernous in a saffron cloud. A fierce young American profile under a lurid sky. They haunt me, insist on my sharing in some dark-purple, universal doom.

Pain—why has it come back, piercing and glancing and jagged? Pain like a searchlight. This is what makes me share. Now I see the shadow faces clear. Dear, individual, friendly faces... as if they could ever grow spectral.... As if I could ever forget Lucinda's soft look under her blue veil. I shall recognize you in eternity, Gertrude, by the sparkle of your glasses and the radiance of your heart....

"I was wounded in the house of my friends."

THE CITY OF CONFUSION

December 4

LORS, il va venir?"

"Who's coming?"

"Veel-son!"

Even the *femme de ménage,* wrinkled and fat old sibyl, has that fact in the front of her consciousness.

She stands where the light falls full on her many shades of bulging, striped-blue calico, watching the doughboys hobble by.

"Pauvres gars! He'll come and visit them. That's what Presidents do. Visit the men they have maimed and ruined for life. (Why did their mothers send them so far, Madame? I wouldn't do as much.) But they say he's different from the other rulers, Veel-son. What does Madame think? *Moi—*" a shrug indicating that all rulers are alike.

Now she is on her knees, absorbing everything she encounters on the floor (a scrap of paper, a match, dust) into her grey cloth, wringing it into the pail, and returning it to the floor with a vicious slop. The only way to prevent her from talking incessantly is to shut your eyes and pretend to sleep. I feel so happy to-day that I can't do otherwise than look at the world and smile. Yellow roses like Florence in May... Yellow mimosa like Mediterranean roads between high walls...

"Madame is better, at last. That's easily seen! Ah, Madame, there were days when you were grey as my cloth "horrible comparison!" I said to my daughter, 'She won't come out of it, *la dame*.'"

Yes, there were days. But this morning, when my nurse pulled back the door of my wardrobe to get a blanket, an almost familiar face looked at me from the mirror instead of a grim stranger. I don't dare say it, but I feel *well!*

The flow of conversation goes on.

"Eh bien, madame, s'il y a des petits boches qui resteront en France, it y *aura des petits francais en Allemagne,"*... looking at me meaningly—*"et des autres Puissances aussi!...* The Boches women, they like Frenchmen much better than Boches. That's funny, eh? I was talking yesterday with a prisoner just back. He told me... Well, the Boches are brutes. Frenchmen aren't like that..." She stopped short, and the subtle shadow of a memory passed over her poor, scrubby old face. Light and mysterious and colored as a butterfly's wing and gone as quickly.... *"Les americains non plus ils ne sont pas brutaux...Ils sont chics, les americains!"*

Who knows what further revelations on the subject of the *"Puissances"* in the Rhineland I should have had if Miss O. had not appeared just then with my steaming bath water. She luckily can't understand a word the scrubwoman says (won't even try to learn French because it "would be no use in Dakota") and thinks her "such a good old lady."

Miss O., too, gives the heartiest welcome to my new feelings of health, and her face shines with sympathy for me when she lifts my cast gently, gently, and there is only a bearable twinge. My sudden release from the intense subjective repression pain insists on will mean a lot to my nurse, too. I shan't be such an " interesting " patient from now on, but ever so much more sociable if I don't have to hold on to myself so tight all the while—if I am really freed from this iron-bound cell.

Apparently in the little hospital world, with its mixture of French and American nurses, the *Entente* has been revived on the warmest terms by the prospects of the President's arrival. The transition stage, since the Armistice, between the cycle of Danger and Death and the cycle of Peace and Reconstruction has been trying in Paris. Nerves were all unstrung and nobody knew the meaning of the cryptic words written so large on the sky. Peace! Nobody knows yet, but one may believe the best, for something is going to happen at last: Wilson is coming!

While she brushes my hair I read Miss O. selections from the President's address to Congress, on the eve of his departure, published in this morning's *Herald.*

The gallant men of our armed forces on land and sea have conscientiously fought for ideals which they know to be the ideals of their country. I have sought to express these ideals; they have accepted my statements of them as in substance their own thoughts and purpose, as the associated Governments have accepted them. I owe it to them to see to it as far as in me lies that no false or mistaken interpretation is put upon them.... It is now my duty to play my full part in what they offered—their lives, their blood to obtain.

So far, so good. The Republican Congress criticises him for not being explicit about what his "full part " implies. But he very well knows, we very well know, I tell my attentive listener, to what he is committed in the hearts of the liberals of the world....

A knock—the doctor! My nurse displays a transformed patient, and he, after one rather surprised glance, sits down astride the white chair, puts his boots on the rounds and his plump chin on the back, lights a cigarette, twists his stubby brown moustache, and begins, while little devils of humor play across his face, to inveigh against "that great and good man President Wilson." Sitting up in my turn against my pillows I feel for the first time in nearly two months an ardent need for controversy. It seems to me I have done nothing but *listen* since October 19th—listen very literally for dear life, to prevent the dark, silent waters of oblivion from closing over my head. Now I am afloat on the stream again, I want to *talk!* I want to answer back!

The doctor, a Francophile *convaincu,* reads the official reactionary press and echoes every view: there is no safety for France save in a permanent system of military alliances; Germany must be completely crushed; the League of Nations is a pipe-dream; Wilson is a Utopian whom most of America does not follow, anyhow, coming over to meddle in subjects too big for him. I, a Franco-phile *convaincu* of another school, deny everything with fury. Quote in rebuttal Jouhaux of the C.G.T., who says Wilson's words—his alone in any governmental office—have gone straight to the heart of the masses. "In opposition to a *paix a la Bismarck,* which would only be a break, a halt before the inevitable recurrence of the horrors we have just endured, rises *la paix Wilson,* radiant, within our grasp..."

"My dear woman, you don't believe a word of it. You are much too intelligent. Have a cigarette?... Come, now, un *peu de courage!"*

Miss O., who has been sitting stiffly by, jaw dropping at our lively exchanges, gapes still further when I accept. And the doctor looks at me as if I were not a patient, but yes—a human being he hasn't noticed before.... I return the compliment and observe him through the cigarette smoke. He is—well, perhaps ten years younger than I had given him credit for... not over forty?... War service makes heavy lines.... I must stop addressing him in a fatherly manner.... He resents it.... Eternally a beau, like all Southerners.... (Though he looks, in that white hospital gown in which he lolls and expands, absurdly like a *bourgeoise en peignoir.)*

What a gifted *raconteur!* He is laying himself out to amuse me—and himself: conjures up the Carolina of his childhood, the Georgia of his youth, the French front of his prime—backgrounds, people, characteristics, warmed with Southern sentiment and seasoned with a large pinch of Gallic salt. We have got to the anecdote of a "nigger" from Georgia who had volunteered in the French Army at the instance of his friend the

King of the Fiji Islands, when an irate surgical nurse pushes open the door.

Her eye unfortunately falling on the cigarette stubs, she turns very red and inquires whether Dr. M. has forgotten his dressings? His operation? He gives me a sheepish look that conceals a sparkle of triumph. (It is good for these women to wait around for a Man. He had kept 'em guessing for two hours by using me as a refuge.)

"Au revoir, monsieur. I'll convert you to Wilson yet!"

"Jamais de la vie!"

Miss O.'s nose seems to be a little out of joint. She brushes up the ashes with an injured and disapproving air, and, when I make no comment, remarks that the doctor will have to learn to make his social calls in the afternoon.

Right from the point of view of your routine, my dear. On the other hand, if a perfect patient is a passive piece of hospital furniture, then—I begin to see—my days of perfection are numbered.

Afternoon

THE most heavenly rest I can remember after lunch. I went to sleep and woke up with the still amazing sensation of being afloat on the river of life, instead of struggling to keep eyes and ears above water; and savored my hospital tea as if it were a meal at the Tour d'Argent. In the midst of it Corinna ushered in, seeming, the straight vivid creature, with her glowing cheeks and bright, melting, friendly eyes and her heaps of abounding gifts, to hail from some halcyon clime—one of those lands of peace and plenty that make the background of old Italian pictures. Is it only that I now see clearly, instead of through a medium of cloudy or feverish feelings, or is America really a halcyon land?

Sue, who soon followed her in, hasn't yet found just the right niche in the Y.M.C.A.; a little regrets important work at home. But Corinna was crowned with her glorious French achievement, and wore the usual scalps at her belt. She was fresh from the liberated North, reeking with its woes, full of plans for the Children of the Frontier, projecting a trip to Germany with General Pershing.

Franco-American comparisons obtrude themselves, these days, as they did in 1917. Then because it was the beginning. Now because it is the end. Two French women have just been here, Madame P. H., wife of my friend the writer on labor subjects, and Mademoiselle G., a nurse high up in the French *Service de Sante,* who after four years in the war zone still directs a group of military hospitals. Madame P. H., a delicious little shy French flower plucked in a cottage garden—pink and white and demure, with a perfume of rare gentleness and sweetness; Mademoiselle G., just the opposite type: a plain, independent, middle-aged spinster, big-boned, big-hearted, progressive, and a feminist.

I can't help contrasting their air of immemorial patience—even the younger woman has it—with Corinna's keen edge of vitality. Even among American nurses who have served with the allied armies—

women like Miss Bullard—there is probably not one whose stoicism and whose responsibility can compare with Mademoiselle G.'s. As for Madame P. H., she has—incredible in so fragile and home-keeping a creature—experienced in her own person the very horrors about which Corinna has talked so eloquently. She has been a "refugee," driven from a stricken city in the North, holding two little children by the hand, another coming, leaving behind a husband mobilized, a house, all her earthly possessions....

Yes, the war service of French women stands out as inevitable, prosaic, planted in fortitude. Whereas our overseas service, at least, is something we have gone to seek—a high adventure. Our American women have, by and large, contributed the same element the American soldiers have to the war—moral stimulus, physical vitality, a new constructive approach to a worn subject, a disbelief in obstacles. But our work, even at its most unselfish, has not been a sacrifice. The palms of martyrdom go to our French sisters.

December 6

THE boundaries of my narrow world are beginning to bulge and crack. I have had my first afternoon out of bed. They lifted me on to the *chaise longue* and wrapped me up and I stayed with the doors wide open for two hours—the idea is to get strength and confidence enough to try crutches on Christmas Day—watching the little garden cosmos of tents, and wounded doughboys, and hurrying nurses. How easily and effectively it turns on its own axis—so indifferent to one's wretched private miseries. But how damp and forlorn the tents are.... I had almost forgotten....

I was accosted from the garden door by a mutilated Blue Devil from the Grand Palais who had a collection of hideous souvenirs made out of copper shell-cases to sell. He had only one leg and part of a jaw, and told me he was going to manifest for Wilson and the *Societe des Nations* with the *Federation Ouvriere des Illutiles* and the C.G.T.

He had the *Populaire* in his pocket, and pointed out with a bitter twist of his cheek this passage: "A man is coming who has kept in the terrible drama a pitiful heart, a right conscience, a clear brain.

We salute him and we say: 'Be faithful to yourself. You have wanted to win to be just. Be just.'"

December 13

IMPOSSIBLE to think of anything but the *George Washington*, drawing nearer and nearer to the coast of France. The French working class, the Socialists, the "people" as distinguished from official France, seem determined to give Wilson a mandate in their cause. Politics are mixed up in it, but the *cri de coeur* is unmistakably there too. The *Journal du Peuple* says: "No man since Jesus, not even Jaures, has so strongly embodied the hope of the world. For the peasant, as for the man of letters, for the workman and the artist this name represents divine Wisdom."

December 14

GUNS! That means ten o'clock. Wilson is arriving at the little station in the avenue du Bois. More guns! He is embracing M. Clemenceau and M. Poincare. More guns! He is starting to drive down the Champs Elysees through the soldiers and the enormous crowds, and the flags....

How can I bear to be here? Scarcely a patch of white cloud on the blue garden sky. The hospital feels lonely and deserted, as on Armistice day. I sent Miss O. to try to see the President. I miss her awfully. I wish she would hurry and get back.

At least the postman goes his rounds. Louise, the concierge, whose rotund, competent countenance now sometimes appears at my door, brings a letter from Rick—raging and champing at Brest, waiting for a transport—to describe yesterday's landing. He saw it from the dock-side where he got a military job for that purpose, and writes of salutes, of Breton peasants by the thousands—"silent, not very interested save when a bit drunk"—of German prisoners throwing down their work to run and stare across the dirty water at the man in the silk hat and fine clothes who is so greatly to influence their destiny.

"The President himself very fine. I wondered just what thrill he had seeing his ugly army men, long straight lines of them down every street, (Americans being the ugliest race on earth, but a great lot, a great and wonderful lot.) He was stirred—obviously. I did not think it possible to show such emotion as he showed with such a fine restraint and dignity. His silk hat, waved only slightly, was more moving and more moved than a whole body's gesture of a Bernhardt. Was he seeing the French as well, or only us? Us, I am certain—just as I could 'hear' his wife's trite comments on the quaint Breton cap.

"We've been dancing—the peasants and some drunken quartermasters—on the bandstand in the square—now *place Président Wilson*—all evening. Even Brest, hole that it is, is gay. Peasants in gorgeous gala still parade the streets in automobiles, passing the hat as they go—alas—in honor of the President!"

My nurse is here, breathless and dazed and happy to have been squashed in the crowd, and trampled on by soldiers. She managed to rent a stool for a large sum from one of the "profiteers" and saw the President's smile. Every one is talking of his smile—as if the poor man had been expected to weep. But Paris is so little given to heroics, so prompt to ridicule the least pompousness in a celebrity, that Wilson's bearing must have been perfect to arouse this extraordinary enthusiasm.

A visit from Lippmann, Merz, R. Hayes, just at supper-time. They were in hilarious spirits, laughing at my efforts to eat my dull meal and also swallow the far more important gist of their remarks. W. L. fairly uplifted. He says the popular feeling came incredibly out of the depths, that Wilson seemed to meet it just as it was given, as if he did realize it was not offered to him as a marl, but to the ideas for which he stands.... To the promise of reorganization for the poor old European world.

The day has been strangely mild and sweet, something like a breath of spring coming in the night windows still. France was the first to say in 1914, "we are making the war against war." They had practically stopped believing it, but now... there are thousands of people in Paris to-night who almost again believe the war has been fought for something bigger than national preservation....

December 16

THE press continues to jubilate over Wilson and he to be feted in the streets.

But I have heard one dissenting voice at last and that in an unexpected quarter: Tom's. He came out late this afternoon to bring me a book and said the President's hash was settled for him. No, he hadn't seen any of the festivities, hadn't (scornfully) cared to, but *happened* to be in an office on the rue de Rivoli when Wilson went by from the Hotel de Ville. He was kissing his *gloved* hand to the crowds! "A terrible omen," said Tom, with a disgusted laugh and a critical gleam.

As if divining my query at his scepticism, he reminded me of the summer evening during the air-raid period, when we had explored the working-class region beyond the place de la Nation. Every house, every shop, was closed and empty in the quarters of the well-to-do—who had fled to safer regions; but here life seethed and teemed, unquenchable and voluble and unafraid. Men, women, and children thronging everywhere. *Bistros* full of gesticulating customers. Family groups seated on the sidewalks. In one street, badly hit by a raid two nights earlier, a friendly baker indicated a warehouse burnt down, three houses smashed in, a wall under which seven people were crushed, a sidewalk from which they had had to dig a woman, embedded like a fly in amber.

Yet only one local shop had closed up, and some wit, voicing the general sense of mankind, had written on the shutters in chalk: *"Fermee par cause de frousse"*—in similar American argot: "He got cold feet."

"Fermée par cause de frousse!" Tom chuckled again at the recollection. If the Germans had marched into Paris, these were the only Parisians who wouldn't have budged. And now it was these people who were the great backers of Wilson against powers and potentates they completely mistrusted. Let the President beware of kid-glove sentiment! Let him beware of giving a sign of *la froussel.*

Tom is desperately restless and abstracted—just as much so as Rick was, really—and wants more than ever to get away from Paris which, he says, is losing its wistful, war-time charm without regaining its peace-time glamour. You can no longer see the town from end to end in one doting glance—as last summer, when it was empty as Pisa—because a hybrid mass of foreigners obstruct the vistas. Turks in turbans on the steps of the Madeleine! Generals of every hue and nation! And—worse—smooth, opulent, possessive, elderly civilians with decorations in their button-holes who wave bunches of twenty-franc notes like so many carrots before the noses of the already baulky taxi-drivers. Hard to hold down a job...

"Where do you want to go?"

"Russia! Germany! Any old revolutionary place! Life here is too much like a book. Interesting but unreal. And it'll be more and more so when the diplomats get going. (You'll see, the Peace Conference will be true to the form of all Peace Conferences!) I want to get into the mess itself. Up to the *ears*.... I want to wander over the face of Europe—for about fifteen years.... That might be enough..." (He has forgotten all about his listener now and his keen, sandy gaze is far-away.) "What interests me is just simply—the world! The divers ways in which men live, produce, eat, think, play, and create.... That's where everything leads you.... New Republic, politics, problem of Middle Europe, science of economics....

"I want a big job to tackle.... There ought to be some for a young man, especially if the old order is gone.... Well, I'll be sure to tell you whether it is or not," he added with a smile and a flash of mending spirits. "We're not going to let you miss anything just because you have a few broken bones!... "

Tom has been a great support through the thick and thin of war Paris. I shall miss him badly. His warm human curiosity, his almost novelist's sense for life, his frankness and his irony. He is changing—something steely and detached is replacing his boyish faiths. Yet I trust his intelligence and his heart. His personal reactions are somehow involved with the bed-rock of the universe. As the universe is now disrupted, he has to go and look down the cracks. Of course. All the more that (through no fault of his own) he missed the great experience of the war—the fighting. Though he doesn't believe in war as a solution for the world's troubles, and knows he has, in his humane food-office, been more closely in touch with its issues—trade, economic balance in Europe—than our common friend Rick, floating high over No Man's Land, he still feels a little cheated, a little reproached by his immunity from danger. He needs "to get into the mess." Hoover ought to manage it.

December 19

THE King of Italy is now being welcomed, in a dismal rain, with—the *femme de menage* assures me—a very skimpy number of salutes. She listened jealously as they were going off, concerned for America's honor, and nodded with satisfaction when it was over: Wilson wins!

December 20

THIS morning she hastened to report the opinion of her daughter, the postal clerk, who went to the station to see the King arrive. Most inferior exhibition. Only one row of soldiers! "*Je t'assure, maman,' qu'elle m'a dit, 'c'etait quelconque, it n'y avait pas deux haies.'*"

My eyes turn only in two directions to-day: towards a pair of crutches standing in the corner; towards the window which reveals lame doughboys walloping along the garden paths as if crutches were no possible impediment.... I shall be leaving the hospital soon, after all....

Cessation from pain is a very positive emotion. The psychology of the New Testament miracles is sound. The God who restores you to these common functions—usually so unthankfully taken for granted—of sight, hearing, locomotion, is really the Saviour of the world. This is what gives doctors their position of almost divine arbitration. There is nothing I would not do for mine, or my nurse, so patient and so homesick as Christmas approaches. (She read me a letter from the Dakota farm to-day about the fall butchering.)

Joffre was yesterday received into the French Academy, and M.'s account of it, and the report of his speech in the *Debats,* has set the Franco-American chord to twanging, clear and far. All the way to Boston Common where I first saw the bluff, serene old soldier—who in so many ways recalls our own Grant—lifted on the tide of

America's violent devotion to France. How remote that exalted spring of 1917 already feels.... "It seemed to the American people that by sheer force of love they would instantly accomplish something great and comforting for the relief of the allied armies." (In French the prose has the noblest classic ring.) "And they were right: this love was to allow France, overwhelmed by the hard trials of the Spring of 1917, to keep her confidence and her courage intact."

It used to seem to me, a year ago, when the early detachments of the A.E.F. and the A.R.C. were arriving in France, that the two countries were exactly in the position of two lovers who had become engaged by correspondence and were meeting for the first time in the flesh. Feelings were brimming over, but fashions of dressing and conducting the business of life were mutually strange and disconcerting.

Theoretically the French themselves desired to be converted to the new American fashion. Our confident youth, our fertility of invention, our vast material prosperity, our efficiency and our scientific method became as lyric a theme as "Wilsonism" is now. But let us hope some lover of the *comedie humaine* made notes of the actual encounter between the French manufacturer who pointed with pride to a factory unchanged since his grandfather's day and the American capitalist who asked when he was going to tear it down; between the New York business man, accustomed in five minutes' telephone conversation to start a train of events to culminate within a week, and the French administrative official who had not abandoned his habit of long-hand letters, long, polite conversations, and long-deferred decisions; between the French peasant who made his toilet in the barnyard, kept his gold in a stocking, and lived frugally on vegetable soup in a house inherited from a revolutionary ancestor, and the sergeant from Ohio, with a cheque-book in his pocket, brought up in an apartment on enamelled bathtubs and beefsteak; between the *poilu,* with his *pinard,* and his resignation, and his pay of five sous a day, and the American private who found his dollars scarcely sufficient to storm the biggest town near his camp on a Saturday night, and drive

French Colonels from their accustomed chairs to make way for his fizzing champagne.

The question is, as the Conference draws near, how much understanding have we achieved through these various contacts and trials? How much even by dying side by side? The first outburst of love between America and France, as Joffre recalls, brought us into war. The second, whose magnetic waves have been radiating from Wilson's smile into the remotest French country- side, is to bring us into peace. But when it comes to the application of Wilson's doctrine, such cheerful remarks as M. Gauvain's in the *Debats* leave one gasping:

"The better we know him the more do we realize that his mind, *though different in formation from ours,* is close to ours. There is reason to hope that our methods, *apparently divergent,* will adjust themselves to our common purposes.... "

Christmas Night

IF I were Amy Lowell I should write a free-verse poem about Christmas Day in the American Hospital. All pictures.

Little French nurses flitting in and out, like pigeons on blue wing. *"Heureux Noel!"* Dakota sails more leisurely, plump and white and starched, from mistletoe to holly. Roses and mimosa and heaps of ribboned bundles. A pair of silver earrings, and crutches in the corner.

"Now for it," says the Head Nurse. She stands by, a little mocking, critical, and earnest. Now for it. Can I? Good. A bit wobbly. "Get her foot up again." The cast weighs a thousand pounds. A million fierce prickles run up my leg like ants, and bite and seethe and bicker in a red-hot ankle.

The doctor makes a fine salute, and eyes the Christmas bottle. *Vieux Marc,* with a doggerel Christmas rhyme about its neck. He listens, till his eyes grow moist. Grabs it, and hurries out.

"Merry Christmas and cheers from Brest, now and forever apparently. Gawd damn." Classic voice of the A.E.F. Merry Christmas from Dijon and Ernest in an equally loud Western voice that fills my room to brimming. Flowers, chocolates, and enormous boots, stowed anywhere at all. Christmas dinner sits lightly on a tray. "Take half my turkey. All my plum-pudding." (Nothing fills him up. His eyes stay hungry.) *"I miss them too. Horribly.* Let's talk about Nancy." But visitors come streaming in, with sherry, and cigarettes, and chocolates.

"Encore du chocolat?" comments the little *chasseur* with scorn. "Will President Wilson feed it to the Germans?"

The door ajar on Christmas plants, set in a row. Holly rustling. Doughboys snoring in their tents, under their comfort bags. My mood flows out to meet and share their dreams of home. On into Paris. On and on to the confines of the earth. And then still on, drawing strength and goodness from some bottomless world-reservoir.

December 30

I AM beginning to be worried by Wilson's apparent unawareness of the complete divergence between his views and those of Clemenceau. Is it unawareness or deliberate ignoring? The President told our troops on Christmas Day that he did not find in the hearts of the great leaders with whom he was associated any difference of principle or fundamental purpose. And now that he is in London, feted and adored and acclaimed again, he seems to have mounted—above the Guildhall—to the crest of a still rosier cloud, whence he waves his silk hat and speaks even more nebulous humanities. It is a strange thing to see Clemenceau craning a stiff neck to this cloud, from the firm soil of *la patrie* and responding with chiselled particularities. The dialogue may be thus abridged from the morning papers:

Wilson: "Our soldiers fought to do away with the old order and establish a new one which will bring honor and justice to the world."

Clemenceau: "From most ancient times peoples have rushed at one another's throats to satisfy appetites or interests."

Wilson: "The centre of the old order was the 'balance of power,' maintained by jealous watchfulness. We must now have, not one group set against another, but a single overwhelming group of nations, trustees of the peace of the world."

Clemenceau: "There was an old system, which appears to be condemned to-day by very high authorities, but to which I am not ashamed to say I remain partially faithful: the balance of power. The guiding principle of the Conference is that nothing should happen, after the war, to break up the alliance of the four powers which together won the victory."

Wilson: "The foundations are laid. We have accepted the same great body of principles. Their application should afford no fundamental difficulty."

Clemenceau: "With old materials you cannot build a new edifice. America is far from the German frontier. Never shall I cease to have my gaze fixed on the immediate satisfaction of the claims to which France is entitled."

Wilson: "It was this incomparably great object that brought me overseas... to lend my counsel to this great—may I not say final?—enterprise of humanity."

Clemenceau: "I may make mistakes, but I can say, without self-flattery, that I am a patriot. France is in an especially difficult situation. *La question de la paix est une question terrible."*

What is "France" to this powerful, little old sceptic? An ancient, intricate, delicately adjusted toy that he holds in his wrinkled hands? Rather, a mistress, whom he clutches to his passionate old heart. His accent, when he speaks of her—again and again through this speech in the *Chambre*—makes Wilson seem, by comparison, to be holding "humanity" at arm's length.

There is a rumor that Lloyd George has won a complete victory for England against the Fourteen Points on the question of freedom of the seas. And the Ebert Government is tottering....

January 1, 1919

THE spirit of the new-born year of victory is a very unrestful one in Paris. Many friends—some I had not seen for a long while—

turned up to wish me well. All, whether men or women, soldiers or civilians preparing to rush to the ends of the earth—to Germany, the Balkans, Syria. The U.S.A. is the rarest of their destinations.

The cumulative effect is that some cog that fixed their rightful place in the scheme of things has slipped. It is the same impression I had at the time of the Armistice intensified: humanity—especially American humanity—cast adrift into space. They all seem hurtling through universal emptiness, their one directing thought to get *somewhere else;* to arrive where a new kind of adventure flourishes; where life is again a highly spiced dish; where they can prolong the war or, better, forget that it is over.

Of course I exaggerate. I am so vowed to endurance and so rooted in the rue Chauveau that all this uneasy movement is disturbing. My own longing is to get out of hospital, home to the United States—away from Europe, from disintegrated people, back to familiar, quiet faces and a desk by a window on a land that has not known war. But the war doesn't happen to be over for me with the New Year, any more than it was with the Armistice. Dr. M. now admits that he has been deceiving me about dates. I have got to stay right here for—well, Miss Bullard frankly says, for three or four months. She, at least, knows I can stand the truth, and told me the French surgeon's view that I shall always have a stiff ankle.

Miss Bullard's tents are finally closed, and she is on her way home. It was wonderful to see her, and hear news of the *blesses,* but rather heart-breaking. The almost fourth-dimensional sense of power and service which sustained such women is gone. They are physically and nervously drained to the dregs, yet they don't dare to stop and rest; that means reflection. Tom's departure to Belgrade was a more cheerful thing to witness—he came to say good-bye—for though he seems somewhat shell-shocked, like everybody else, the pinnacle of life is still before him—war to him was not the pinnacle. Whereas the nurse feels as the aviator did that she can never again find such a peak as she has climbed in the last years.

A curious phenomenon I have been noting in the American men: those under forty, even if ready to go home, almost universally wish to find new jobs. The ones they had before the war were, they say, unsatisfactory. Now is the time to change. Often they propose to seek not only new occupations, but new American habitats. This is so marked a masculine reaction that I was surprised when my old English friend, F. E., who for four years has been an ordnance officer in Flanders—and turned up delightfully on leave—told me he was "going back to the cotton business." British phlegm? Perhaps not, as the business is now in Egypt!

The doctor came in to see me this evening, the picture of desolation, all the lines of his face slanting down instead of up. It does not do for a man of the *bon vivant,* gather-ye-roses temper to look either backward or forward at the New Year, especially after the shades of forty have closed in. The present is the only safe ground, and when it fails under the feet, as Paris is about to fail for Dr. M.... Why is it that humorists and storytellers whose particular gift is to make others laugh have so underlying a sadness, and why arc cynics so sentimental?

To-night the doctor was unhappy because he hadn't written to his mother—hadn't and *couldn't.* He tells me that all at once, during the war, after prolific letter-writing, he ceased to be able to set down a line. He is rather proud of his queer inhibition, but also oppressed by self-reproach towards his Southern friends and especially towards this dear old lady, whom he thinks " the most charming woman in the world." She sounds like my grandmother, with an aroma of the Waverley Novels about her. He finally cheered up, tucked himself into the *chaise longue* under a steamer-rug, as if for a sea voyage, and launched forth into a variegated version (by no means a Walter Scott version) of his past romantic adventures. I told him that if he weren't more careful I should be writing his autobiography.

Deliver me, o God of Battles, from pity for other people or myself! That is the best New Year's prayer I can formulate. The men who were killed do not want our pity or need it. They gave their lives so eagerly and freely, the first of them, so awarely and impersonally, the last of them—clear-eyed young figures like Stewart—that we are unworthy of them if we offer it. And surely the survivors are not to be pitied, but envied for their chance to put a great experience to lifelong use. The way we shall measure warriors and war-workers in the future, I am sure, is by their ability to get away from the war, to make it merely the foundation of a new existence. The ones who live constantly in memory of it will be the same futile type of human creature who is always harking back to golden college years.

If only I could go home. The Paris scene has suddenly lost the brightness which Wilson's coming brought. It is murky, and confused, and haunted, and the ghostly voices that wail over the city to-night offer an ominous welcome to 1919.

January 2

A NEW world has dawned for me: the hospital outside my room. I have been practising in my own small domain, and to-day had the terrific adventure of walking on crutches down the long, slippery corridor, assisted by my anxious Miss O., while the whole surgical and nursing force gathered to applaud and jeer. Dr. M. is a terror on these occasions, sends the nurses into hysterics, and goads the patient to unparallelled effort—exactly what he wants. Even Simon, the husband of the concierge, a sloping-shouldered, chipper little Frenchman in blue jeans, took his place in the group, and with that instinct for hard fact that never fails the French workman said, "*Allez, mademoiselle,* when spring comes you'll see how your luck will turn!" "When spring comes..." I wanted to hear, "You'll be leaving us next week!"

The corridor is narrow and dark, and I turned the corner into a very bright gallery which is entirely glass, opening on the garden. There stands the white table of the floor-nurse, with her records: there stand a few inviting wicker chairs (into one of which I was assisted, with trembling knees); and there, above all, on a white bed that seems to grow out of banks of flowers, with a big blue bow on her bobbed black hair, and the vividest of dark eyes, lies one of the most charming young French girls I have ever seen.

My nurse has been telling me much about "Mademoiselle V."—how she has been in the hospital since May—that is some eight months—under the care of the Red Cross, with an abscess of the lung due to careless throat treatment in a hospital when she was nursing our soldiers. How she is quite alone in the world, deserted by her French family because she refused to marry the young man of their choice. How she is the *enfant gatée* of the American Hospital, the friend of the little nurses, the darling of the doctor, the doughboys' delight. How she is often in pain and feverish; how she sometimes cries; how she may never recover, but is intensely social, and manages to stop every one on the way to the rooms beyond; nurses, doctors, visitors, caught by her perfume as bees are attracted by a flower, forced by her sweetness to give her attention, and kindness, and gifts, and news of the world.

So, of course, she knew about the wounded American woman. She had heard the rumpus stirred up by Dr. M. and was waiting eagerly for me to appear. When I had drunk Miss O.'s sherry, I was helped to a seat beside her and we had a little talk: about New Orleans where she was brought up (that may account for her revolt from French family tradition) and France where she was born. She came back just before the war, and doesn't know which country she loves better. She speaks with great vivacity, with the prettiest gestures of her plump and rounded arms, while the curves of her cheeks flush red out of a skin warm as a white pearl. She radiates health, one would say—something supremely good and sane as well as supremely alluring. But over her pillow hovers a shadow. Where had I seen that shadow before?... Fate... Disaster... I last saw it over the heads of the young soldiers. How blind to suppose that the end of the war had placed timeless youth beyond the reach of that dark wing!

As I got up to start laboriously homeward I caught sight, through a glass partition into an adjoining room, of an old man in bed: a bald, shiny head with a few sprigs of white hair; a face hollowed like a skull with its chin bound in bandages. Miss O. replied to my question that he is a Welshman (she thinks) and a professional jockey, dying of cancer of the face. And added, in lurid detail, what it was like to do his dressings and feed him.... The nurses involuntarily turned away.... He smiled at them, even so, and mumbled thanks. No war wound could be more horrible. And he gets, I suspect, none of the moral consolations of the wounded. There wasn't a flower in his room. Miss O. says his only visitor is an old wife, who comes rarely, from a distance.

I have been thinking too long in terms of the wounded. In every civil hospital in the world youth and age must be dying of incurable and ugly disease, with but a glass between them—if we knew or cared back. Small and cramped and picayune. And no longer peaceful since the door fails to shut out the rest of the hospital. Everything I had seen trailed in after me. Seated itself like a hobgoblin on my pillow, and jibbered when I tried to hide my head under the bedclothes.

January 8

RECONSTRUCTION is a miserable business. The reality of learning to walk all over again on two imperfect legs has brought my morale down fifty per cent. I know now just how convalescent soldiers feel, sitting around a stove in a base hospital. The clouds of *ennui* which envelop the tents in the garden have rolled in and filled my room. Meanwhile the Peace Conference covers itself with *a* heavy pall of secrecy and doubt, and the stream of visitors runs dry. The worst week since my accident.

Mary has talked to me a lot of the laziness and inertia of her soldier patients. They won't bend stiff knees; won't try to hobble with sticks. Obviously the reason they won't is that every step a wounded man takes sets up a horrid jar, strain, wrench, or ache somewhere. And even if he does stiffen his moral courage and resolve to be excruciated, his energy quickly lands him in a physical prohibition: however hard he works it is going to take months and months, years and years, perhaps, to get that foot or knee back to real use, and he will be physically depleted the whole time. So why worry? Why not sit by the stove?

The only thing that prevents is a certain sort of intelligent determination—and the arm of a nurse to lean on. I am luckier than the doughboys in having one usually at hand. Even so, every snail-like progress down the corridor is as difficult as an ascent of the Matterhorn. I thought I was going to be able to do some real work once I was up, but my time is spent in making a stupendous effort, recuperating from it and beginning again. Like the tide on the beach. Only it looks to me, on this long grey afternoon, as though I should never reach the fringe of grass at the high edge of the sand.

January 10

I HAVE been walking—call it that—in the garden, assisted by chairs, benches, crutches, sticks, and a nurse. The garden must really have been pretty in pre-war days, with its great trees, and its flower-beds, its pebbled alleys and rococo embellishments which date back to the time when our hospital was the abode of some mistress of Louis Philippe. But now the damp, floppy, grey-brown tents squat heavily there—like patient dachshunds or a discouraged circus. The alleys are trodden out by hobnails and smeared with mud from the overflowing Seine, and the clustered doughboys have scarcely the spirit to smile.

The only cheerful person we met was a very young fellow with a dancing pair of black eyes, dressed in a nondescript American uniform, whom I supposed to be of the A.E.F., till he spoke to me in French. How did he happen to be here? *"Mon oncle d' Amerique."* The American comrades had taken him in, were clothing him, feeding him, lodging him, giving him cigarettes and chocolate, and the American *major* was dressing his wounds. *Chic,* eh? He was jubilant over escaping French army red tape. What would he do when the doughboys left? Time enough to think of that when they really did go—they had been on the point of it so long. *"Je me debrouillerai toujours."* No mistaking that *poilu* accent.

The hospital might look very pleasant on a bright spring morning, red brick, white trimmings, glass galleries. Under to-day's lowering sky the glass revealed only human misery. First we crawled by the diet kitchen: three nurses quarrelling for possession of the stove; then by the long gallery: Mademoiselle V. lying wan, with closed eyes. Next we sat down on a bench and looked up at the sun parlor on top of the house, now a Red Cross convalescent ward: six or eight women extended in dejected attitudes, or putting on their stockings.

I begged Miss O. to take me away from hospital sights. So we tried an unfrequented path at the back of the garden. It was lined with shrubs with shiny green leaves and had that bosky and melancholy charm, that luscious earthy smell which I have breathed at Versailles in winter. The good smell of the earth after so long indoors! But Miss O. shivered, and thought the high walls that shut us in from the adjoining estate depressing. She is used to twenty degrees below zero, crisp snow, open fences, wide, sunny horizons, and hates these leaden skies, these oozing brick walls and solemn brick houses behind them which look so "old," and don't always stand four-square to the street. Cities, she announced definitely, are beautiful in proportion as they are new, and geometrical in pattern and, preferably, built of wood.

The wall makes me rebellious. I want to get out, since I have seen it. We painfully made the circuit by the Nurses' Home, past the glass-walled reception-room, full of rows and rows of Y.M.C.A., A.R.C., and K. of C. of both sexes, waiting to consult the doctors. My companion grew—unconsciously—more shivering, bored, and depressed every inch of the way. It is no wonder. She is engaged to a farmer in Dakota. Her letters come very irregularly, and the Red Cross holds out no hope of a speedy release.

The rumors from the Peace Conference are disturbing. I think of it now as a sort of vast, unwieldy ferry-boat which is trying to make the crossing from one shore to another.... The hawsers will not be actually cast off till the 18th, but the pilot is getting up steam, and the bark has begun to heave uneasily. The waves it stirs up are, however, rather spent before they reach the shores of Neuilly. It is not to be supposed that I can get much light from Miss O. on "Bolshevism," or from Mademoiselle V. on "Self-Determination." I asked the hospital house-painter, a smiling, chubby old fellow dressed in a white smock, whom the nurses call *"Pigeon Blanc,"* what he thought about "Indemnities."

"Un tas de Mises, tout ca. La guerre est finie. Travaillons!"

Friends in Paris continue wonderfully kind about taking the long journey to Neuilly. In the last two days visits from F. T., Walter Lippmann, and Pierre Hamp, all of whom I, of course, interrogated on the Conference. F. T. quietly said that outsiders can know nothing, that no opinion is possible. Pierre Hamp scratched his black head and spoke a pungent word against Clemenceau and the imperialists. But since he has been to the Lille region and seen with his ferreting eyes the destruction wrought by the Germans in the factories he knows so well, his passion for industrial recuperation more than ever dominates the rest.

W. L. looks more harassed every time he comes. He now almost despairs of a victory of Wilsonism against special interests and imperialist ambitions. He says France wants it both ways—wants to guard her frontiers heavily and make a defensive alliance against Germany, and yet wants the League of Nations, without accepting its implications of common trust and good faith.

"How I envy you your detachment!" he suddenly burst out.

There spoke the editor! The only type of young American in my experience who longs to go back to his old job is the writer who has been muzzled by the censor, or precipitated into a life of action by the war. His stored reflections are beginning to choke him. W. L. can't wait to get home, out of uniform, back to the N. R. office. When he talked of the office his face began to change, and by the time he had taken some snapshots of his wife out of his pocket it was shining. Like Ernest, he has the best thing America or indeed the world produces in the way of marriage: his wife is a lovely young contemporary who backs him—and is backed—in a destiny of freedom. Those are the marriages that stand the separations of the A.E.F. as the thousands of others one could point to do not. But I shall be glad when the various pairs in which I take an interest are reunited, even though W. L.'s impending departure again makes me feel like the one fixed point in a firmament that is shifting its stars like an August sky.

January 15

My last dressing is over. When the bandages came off to-day the deepest wound had closed—three months, practically, from the accident. Dr. M., very pleased with himself and me, leaned back in his chair, pushed up his grandfather spectacles, and said all that remained to be done was to borrow a large black felt slipper from some benevolent concierge, and put my stiff foot in charge of a "horny-handed Swede"—represented as an ogre who loves to crack the bones of shrieking ladies. This could not take place for a fortnight.

"What are two weeks to you?" he asked, noting my disappointment. "You have years before you to cure that foot in."

So has Northern France years, centuries, to repair her devastation. But both the refugees and I are in a hurry.

January 18

PEACE CONFERENCE officially weighs anchor for parts unknown, threatened—but unshaken—by thunder and lightnings from the American and British press on the subject of "open covenants." Nothing to be given out but a colorless and worthless daily bulletin, agreed on by the principal powers.

January 20

UNEXPECTED visit from the French surgeon who performed my operation at Mont-Notre-Dame. I was glad of the chance to express again my gratitude for his great skill and kindness, but somewhat taken aback by his transformation from the weary, middle-aged, unshaven *toubib* of the black pipe into a dapper, pink-cheeked, correct young man not a day over thirty-five. Very smart blue uniform, very varnished, pointed boots.

He was intensely and genuinely interested, as French surgeons always are, to follow up the results of his work, and admitted it had been a *tour de force* of which he was somewhat proud. He was sorry to miss Dr. M. Might he venture a little advice? Go very, very slow with walking, be very, very courageous about massage, try sun baths (in this weather!) and resign myself to at least four months more of hospital. For his part he was immediately sailing for Africa, to do postwar surgery. Africa... a sudden vision of the inside of an ambulance and two staring Senegalese faces....

January 23

I HAVE been completing my surgical education by watching Dr. M. operate for appendicitis. It was a real event, that seemed to strengthen my legs, and put a sort of foundation under the hospital world. How bloodless and decent the procedure, how delicate and exquisitely sure the hand of science. The doctor's terse comment, as he made his incision through the hole in the sheet, classified the Y man on the table as neatly as the knife cut the skin:

"No muscles? All in his knees, I suppose!"

January 30

THE atmosphere of Paris is chimerical. Every one who comes to see me brings and confirms the impression. The Conference has become a source of deep resentment, for not even the so-called "insider" knows what Clemenceau, and Wilson, and Lloyd George, and Orlando are brewing in their secret still. But the rumor that it is a strong brand of moonshine begins to circulate. "The German colonies are to be divided as plunder." "The League of Nations will not be an integral part of the Treaty." The people just from America are especially aghast. H. G., on her way to an important relief job in the Balkans, described her illusion of a series of concentric circles revolving in a vacuum. The inner circles are, of course, the four great powers, but even they scarcely touch each other in their rotation; and the smaller and oppressed nations turn madly on the circumference. She says people look to her like gnats sucked into this dusty orbit or that, whirled breathlessly round and round.

I see Paris through the wrong end of the telescope, anyhow, which adds to the gnatlike effect. The hospital, in contrast, is presented always more microscopically to my gaze, its *minutice* magnified far more than life-size. With its odd mixture of American Colony and Red Cross standards, its conglomerate medical and nursing staff, its patients who vary from relief workers to ex-ambassadors and peace commissioners, it is a rather extraordinary cross-section of America in France; but one is not constantly in a scientific mood. Both the unanimistic French tent, and the isolation of my very sick period here, were finer than the immersion in petty detail gradually forced upon me by convalescence.

The whole place ends by having glass walls—and every ripple of the goldfishes' tails is revealed. I can't help knowing just how the distinguished statesman next door takes his tea and washes his face, and the secret whispered by Miss X. in the consulting-room is telepathically conveyed to my ears. The sound of a doorbell at midnight, a stifled masculine laugh, a flutter in the corridor—these are no longer meaningless noises, but notes of a very real and healthy existence which goes on inside the hospital, no matter who lives or dies. A sort of violin obligato with an almost cynical resonance, played high above the regions where the Y girl with pneumonia cowers from the spectre at the foot of her bed, and Mademoiselle V. cries miserably for a hypodermic.

She is coughing terribly to-night. I can't bear to hear—pain, and sickness, and wounds... I had accepted them. They gave me a deeper share in the common lot. But the common lot of the European world grows darker and darker. Too many people with coughs and wounds. Too many with no food. Too many to back against Catastrophe and Destiny. Morbid old Europe—Miss O. is right, its walls are too high. Gradually they are growing together overhead, enclosing us in an airless dungeon in which we can only grope, like characters in a Maeterlinck play. Let us get back into the light.

The luminous light that burns on the Arizona desert, out of long miles of untouched sage and sand. Yes, that's where I want to be, on an observation car travelling swiftly into the Southwest. Losing myself in the shimmer of fine dust, passing the bold, red ramparts of a land beloved of pioneers, and large enough to carry Europe in its pocket.

February 3

To dress again for the street; to drive again through the French night; to confront a restaurant, full of lights and people; to sit down at a real table, with a real white cloth, and feast on *canard a l'orange* and escarolle salad, with a real bottle of Burgundy...

The doctor is a sport, and it all felt like a steeple-chase. Involving, in fact, such a breathless series of hurdles as I could never have jumped on crutches but for his urgent and joyously encouraging voice at my back. He had generously decided I "needed a change"—and carried out his decision with lavish efficiency.

It was one of those misty-moisty winter evenings that swallow up landmarks and I strained my eyes in vain from the taxi to discover anything significantly "different" in the dim streets.

Larue's also looked after my first mad dizziness had subsided—much the same as before the Armistice. A pair of boastful young A.E.F. captains at the next table, completely immersed in their grudge against "the major" were, for some occult reason, Dr. M.'s and my best dish. Their native flavor! The bond created between Americans in France by their common Americanism and the share it gives them in every other variety of Americanism is one of the emotions that doesn't seem to have worn out. I can't possibly think of Paris now without *us,* in uniform, overrunning it. What would Henry James say to that?

Hospital quiet was blissful to return to, though. Here, to-day, weary enough in my long chair, my old Harvard friend R. M. J. found me. He too is very tired and worn, but no less full of human spice—and trenchant observation and comment from Chaumont. We took a look down the perspectives of history together, at the revolutionary Europe that is emerging so chaotically from the wreck of the old dynasties. Could it ever be worth the cost of the Great War? Perhaps. The past does bear witness to costs unbearable contributing at last to the onward reach of man. But as to the Fourteen Points the historian said that when the envoys were duly assembled at Spa nobody, not even the Americans, had a copy of them. They had to send to Berlin to get Erzberger's! Another little anecdote: the distinguished American envoy, to the captain-secretary who sits at his elbow in a stage whisper: "The Palatinate? Palatinate? Where *is* the Palatinate?"

To-night my first séance with the Swedish masseur, Mr. M., who proves highly intelligent, indeed an almost delightful person—I wonder if my qualification isn't due to the woe he inflicted the head of a hospital for French war wounded.

Sad survey of my left ankle. Home truths that nearly extinguished hope. Cheering assurance that I shall walk anyhow. Massage. Bending of the unyielding joint a process which sounds and feels very much like an effort to separate the wainscoting from the wall. It brought beads of perspiration to Mr. M.'s forehead and extracted groans from me. This to be repeated every day—indefinitely. Yes, indefinitely. I may as well not blink the fact.

February 4

THE second dose of massage was worse than the first. But its badness has the virtue of making me feel something is doing. Feel that I am again lucky to fall into the hands of a specialist—luckier than most of the thousands of wounded Americans, Frenchmen, Englishmen, Canadians, Belgians, Italians, Serbians, Germans, Russians, who by an awful sort of geometrical progression magnify, pile up my infinitesimal "case " into a tremendous burden for the world's vitality to bear. The masseur has confirmed my fears for the soldiers crippled towards the end of the war. He says that even in France they will be turned out of the hospitals only a quarter cured. Class D... I gather all the under dogs of the universe to my heart, these days....

Harry Greene came just at the right moment to cure me of the psychology of the under dog. His kind, quizzical, New England face, his endearingly familiar Boston quaver, his air—through his faithful eye-glasses—of taking Paris and its mad preoccupations as frivolous and highfalutin and unimportant, compared to the serious, and steady, and unending parochial business of rebuilding Northern France, have given me a new sense of reality. I think of my trips in his Ford in 1917, through the region of ruined villages, and little white crosses, and felled orchards of which he has so long been the faithful servitor. Lettuces sprouting in the shell-holes. Resolute old French folk in the cellars. If Harry went about pitying these inhabitants of the North instead of meeting them in the spirit of pioneering social service he would not be half the wonderful use he is. No place but for stoicism in this devastated world of which we are all citizens. Let us accept our part in the tragedy without expecting moral or physical compensation. "For the greatness of Reason is not measured by length or height, but by the resolves of the mind. Place then thy happiness in that wherein thou art equal to the Gods."

The determination of the various nations to get their "just deserts," their real and final reward of virtue and suffering, is precisely the poisonous element in the Conference. It is that which may yet prevent an effective League of Nations. Wilson's voice is failing, failing, and the voice of self-pity and self-interest is swelling. The ironic idealists, like A. S., who with his wife does so much to make Neuilly happy for me, are beginning to express their doubts. He appeared at my door after lunch—from the garden where he had tied his dog—with a poem which sets forth very plainly what

Le prudent, l' aimable marchand is trying to make out of the war and the peace.

February 5

THE Paris dinner broke a spell. I am now at least half free. To-day the dear and handsome Peggy came, by permission of Dr. M., to spirit me away to lunch with her and Lucinda, and I braved a dining-room full of smart French officers where a certain famous princess—who must be a relative of Queen Mary—was solemnly eating omelette, gnocchi, chop and fruit in immaculate brown kid gloves.

Even a chop hath charm, after lukewarm hospital fare, and so after a hospital room has a "salon"—*the* salon with its German helmets and other trophies, its open fire and flowers, and the two radiant American girls who for so many young officers besides our beloved Stewart have made it a "home from home."

Stewart, of course, was in the front of our thoughts. He had gone forth from the salon so gaily, and never, never more should we see him.... But his charming little philosophic countenance seemed still to regard us from the angle by the fire, charging us not to rarefy or heighten his soldier's end. We might, if we liked (he indicated) remember the fragrance of his roses, and when we drank "Chateau Yquem" pledge him a secret toast....

"Aren't you fascinated by the technique of surgery?" asked Peg, after a pause, and told of a *poilu* with no face to speak of, whose arm was grafted to his forehead, sitting on the edge of his bed singing "Madelon," as he prepared to leave the Ambulance. Peggy had never been so well and happy as while nursing. Lucinda had invented a bandage which they had adopted at Blake's—nothing ever made her so proud. After the wards there were emptied she walked through, seeing the faces of the dead rise from their pillows.... Soldiers and surgery—every effort to discuss purely feminine matters brought us back to them. The orientation of these so-called society girls is perfectly definite. They have seen the best of war—the extraordinary human heroism it calls forth, and the extraordinary skill of science in patching up what science has destroyed. They have seen the worst of war—its suffering and its waste. And it is all so near, so passionately absorbing. Both girls spend their time going to the other end of Paris to console "their" boys—unfortunately now cared for in inferior conditions. The maddening American army—what was the use of the finely weighed and pondered wisdom of Blake's and the Ambulance if nothing was to be carried through, if the rest of the treatment was careless and ignorant?

And what will happen, asked the girls, to these wounded heroes' characters, even if their limbs recover? Much as one adores them, with their grit, their grouch, their young inconsequence, those in Paris at least are spoiled. They are fairly gorged with chocolate by the various rival letters of the alphabet, so much so that they won't eat their regular meals. Refuse to learn handicrafts, as the *poilus* do. Hardly read even a magazine. Just lie around, expecting to be amused and petted, and watching for the "chow" cart in order to damn the contents.

Peggy is shiningly "glad her fate is settled." Her very special officer husband is waiting for his orders, and she, now nursing is over, hates Paris. She went to a dance at the Aviation Club, but didn't enjoy dancing as she did before the war. No fun to dine at a restaurant either, and see a lieutenant spend his last hundred francs on you. No satisfaction (puts in Lucinda) to go to the opera with a peace-maker in a U.S. Government car lined with striped velvet, when Eastern Europe is starving, and your best patient is neglected. The Americans are doing the peace too lavishly. What are the Wilsonians accomplishing?

Stop, stop, my dears... Let me go back to the grey room... As Lucinda leaves me there in my nurse's hands, I can only offer the usual spinster's advice:

“The riddle of the universe doesn’t seem to have been solved by the war. So why not, meanwhile, decide to marry one of the faithful of the salon—for instance...” But she is at the door and gives me only a dark, mysterious, little, goodbye smile.

February 9

ERNEST is about to be transferred to Paris. All through the long, slow spring I shall have this brother-in-law turned brother to count on. I had to-night a foretaste of what it is going to mean when he jollied up the doctor and took me to dine at Prunier’s; and was, I declare, as skilful as the doctor himself in getting me and my crutches to a table.

The table was in the downstairs room less *chic* than the inaccessible upper regions. The only other American a private with a vulgar little French dumpling of a woman, against a brawny shoulder. Beside us in the corner sat a French lieutenant with a really beautiful girl—perfectly dressed, quiet and distinguished. He never took his eyes from her face; every now and then reached across the table for her hand and kissed it. Yet there was delicacy even in this public avowal—every word they spoke, every gesture, his way of consulting her taste in ordering the dinner indicated an intimacy full of fine shades of understanding.

Ernest shrugged impatiently towards our rather offensive fellow-American:

“That bounder,” he said, “is really no different in Paris from what he is at home. It is only that what is there furtive, back-alleyish, has come blatantly out into the open. Perhaps better so. Though he and his kind, with their rotten taste—or lack of taste—give the revolt from Puritanism an unpleasant cast. Almost never does a Frenchman offend good taste.”

I asked to what degree he felt contact with European *mores* had changed the moral standard of American men in general.

“Ah, that’s harder to say... such an individual matter. I know some who have really decided the European way is easier and pleasanter; who really have lost something—if it is a loss, as I believe. Others have merely gone through a crazy phase due to loneliness, overstrain or some other aspect of war and will revert to normal when they get home. But undoubtedly many a rigid Puritan has learned tolerance, and personally I think that is a gain—to discover that standards aren't absolute, that they vary with nations and individuals, that the measure of the rightness of a given relation is, in large part, the quality and beauty of the relation itself. But the ultimate effect on American life and manners?—Who knows...

"I have a pretty definite impression, haven't you"—he went on—"that our *mores* have fundamentally stood the test—and what is more unexpected, justified themselves to the French. There I can speak positively. I see it in Dijon. You know I have made some wonderful friends there. There's one girl—unmarried, of the ancient local aristocracy and two or three years older than I lives with her married sister, Madame S., who is one of the loveliest young women I ever knew. I've got the habit of dropping in often for tea, and they both told me recently that I have made them believe in something they never before thought possible—*amitie* between the sexes, affectionate friendship without sentimental complications.

"Even the young Frenchmen are impressed by our strange ways. At first, of course, they simply couldn't 'get' us at all—us and our Y girls. They thought it was all some sort of a hypocritical fake. But now they believe and rather admire, though some of them simply can't understand how it is possible for a man and a woman to go off for a day's excursion on mere comradely terms, or for a man like myself to have so many close friends among women and still care for only one. But there's D—; he told me he had been having an affair with *a jeune fille* in Dijon. He now thinks it was a mistake, especially for her, and says that he is done with that sort of thing forever.

"But it's the French girls who have been most deeply affected—by watching our independent girls measuring up to their many responsible jobs—and especially by knowing our better types of American men. I can't tell you how many—girls I've met in Paris and Tours and Dijon—have told me, with an air of real sincerity, that they could never go back to idle lives, and could only marry if they married Americans..."

Here our neighbor rose to help his gracious *amie* into her smart black satin cape and Ernest, cigarette in fingers, settled his shoulders back comfortably against the shiny leather cushion for a sympathetic contemplation of the couple. His dark eyes have such wisdom and power—and

I have watched both qualities deepen with each fresh sight of him.

"Well, my dear, it's been a great experience, altogether?"

"Great... yes, subjectively great indeed. Of course, my experience in the S.O.S. has been as different from the fighting soldiers as light from dark. Your friend Rick wouldn't think much of it. But it's just as fine in its way, I maintain. Look here... a Captain I saw yesterday summed it up. He's been the head of an airplane construction plant in some little sandy hole—and he said he felt as if he could go home now and build the Panama Canal single-handed."

"That is indeed the opposite of the fighters' rather disintegrated psychology—their sense of anti-climax."

"Precisely," agreed Ernest. "The S.O.S. gives you a brace for life, whereas after the front life is inevitably anti-climax—for a while anyhow. After my work in the War Risk first, and then in the Intelligence I feel ready to tackle any job, however big—and get away with it, too, you bet. When the Colonel sent me to take over the newly opened office at Dijon he said he didn't know the conditions and could offer no advice. 'Go down and make good.' So I did. No more than every one else. We have all attacked perfectly unknown jobs, without preconceived ideas, with no special tools or qualifications—and made good.' Of course not in terms of absolute success—but in success measured against opportunity offered, yes."

"But weren't there a lot of men with routine jobs,—plain drudgery?"

"To be sure. And they'll go home as dull-spirited and fishy-eyed as they came. Because they didn't have the wits to get transferred, poor beggars. I 'm speaking of men of a higher calibre. And the most thrilling part, for them of course,—if I may still subjectify—the thing that makes the A.E.F. experience different from any other one has had or can have again on this globe, is the *freedom* of it. Freedom from responsibility first."

"But surely there's enormous responsibility in these hard jobs?"

"Such an impersonal responsibility compared to those at home. Nothing to do, once the job is done for the day or week, but wait for your travel orders—and if they aren't forth coming get off without 'em!"

"And then freedom from ties... of course one wouldn't, of one's own volition, drop below the surface of life, and duck off to another world, leaving behind everything one most values. Wife and baby... job, house, and committees... one did it because it was the right thing to do, because one had to take a part with the rest of humanity. But it is nevertheless a precious and wonderful opportunity. Wild as I get with homesickness, I look forward enormously to these coming Paris months... the work and its problems... the infinitude of evenings, Sundays, and long lunch hours and talk. God,—what I've learned about the art and philosophy of *living* in France... Just because, for the first time, I've had leisure to observe... to *savourer lentement la vie...* If only Katharine could get that passport and spend the Spring here it would be complete... but even without her we'll both be the better for it... you understand?"

"I certainly do. It's hard on the wives, but I believe if I were God Almighty organizing a world I 'd include a period like this one of yours in the existence of every young man who like you began to live seriously and responsibly so young—a new field to test his powers, a chance to get his personal and lonely bearing with the universe—before the plateau of thirty, the burdens of a growing family, the Panama Canal!"

"It was a great school for swelled heads too," ruminated Ernest. "We are none of us likely to exaggerate our individual contribution. We see its utter insignificance—except to ourselves."

"But we also begin to see what the sum of our tiny contributions amounted to in the A.E.F. Something pretty big... something to be proud of..."

February 16

THIS is a black night in the rue Chauveau. The Paris of the Americans is all very well till one sees the Paris of the French. I have again been to a literary tea-party on the *quai,* again pushed open the Henri IV door above the Seine and found myself in the salon with the Gauguin over the divan and the Blanche on the left wall, in the presence of a charm and a mystery... France is again *chez elle.*

It is almost the first time since the war that I have seen her so. When I arrived in 1917 her *chez elle* was invaded by foreign hordes, and she was seeking to be hospitable—especially to the Americans. (Was I not lodged in this very room last winter? I can't believe it.) It is perhaps natural that in our crass hotels and hospitals we have not sufficiently taken in the change from war to peace. We are still *transatlantiques,* leading an abnormal, transplanted existence connected with the touristic and suburban regions of this ancient city,—with the blatancies of the Champs Ely-sees and the boulevards, with the monotonies of Neuilly rather than with the intimacies and exclusions of the *rive gauche* and the *Cite.* Our peace Paris differs only in chromolithograph degree from our war Paris. The French war Paris, as M. Jean Giraudoux and I once agreed, was like an 18th Century print—a place of noble architectural perspective, every broad and empty street sweeping upward to some wide-winged Louvre, or colonnaded Odeon. But the French Peace Conference Paris is a painting with all the richness and depth of tone, all the subtleties of value in which that perhaps greatest of French arts abounds. Only a French painter of the first tradition could have rendered that literary *interieur* as I saw it to-day, with its distinguished women in plain black with square-cut necks, its slim *jeune jille* serving tea, its young novelists in picturesque army disguise, and its solemn groups of bearded, black-coated elder gentlemen using the subjunctive tense with care, and never referring to an *Allemand* as a *Boche.*

What made the difference from literary tea-parties of the winter of 1918—the ones where our host was home on leave? It wasn't that he was no longer in uniform, or that the room was really warm—filled with a delicious, diffused heat—or really bright with candle light, and fire light, and flowers. These were contributory factors.

But the cause and centre of the change was spiritual. France had come home. The war was won in her favor, and she had at last retired into her ancient interior, shut her hoary, hand-hewn door and settled to a kind of converse with herself in which the ally of yesterday had no real share. "There are only two civilized nations in the world, the Chinese and the French." Where did I hear that phrase? In this very salon, years ago? It came back to me as I sat in my comfortable chair, listening to the talk of the French *literati.*

A mandarin certainly the intellectualist critic of Bergson whose small, hard, pale visage glooms out of a corner by the fire. A mandarin certainly the tall, emaciated young man with the eyeglass, who writes prose exactly as Debussy writes music, and walks in old Paris like a poet in green fields. Here comes the novelist of the slow, fine smile—his Polish wife in her piquant blue cap smiles too, from afar who cannot romance nowadays until after nine at night. "Till then I belong to all sorts of vague entities—France, internationalism!" He is translating Henry James because he "understands him" although—a distinction worthy of the setting—he doesn't understand English. The black-coated elders seem to be discussing the newest books:

Riviere's *l'Allemand*, the prison record of a literary critic who has discarded the usual reasons for hating the Germans in favor of others more damning; Gasquet's *Hymnes*. The warm Provençal Gasquet... it was he who showed me Verdun... My host approaches with the big volume. "You must read it," he says, "like a symphony."

I was welcomed with all the old kindness—with an added touch of gentle solicitude since this was my first French *sortie.* Little direct mention of Wilson, little of the Conference, less of the Quai d'Orsay. And yet the sense that the peace was going ill was all-pervasive. Why was it going badly? Ah, that was exactly the point. These hypocritical British with their "mandates," these Americans with their ignorance of tradition, and their ten thousand horse-power idealism—were they not combining against France? The mandarins seemed to nod agreement to an Anglo-Saxon Menace. When I got up to proceed to the door again on the arm of my host, and the company rose, bowing, from their dusky corners, I read on those intelligent, sympathetic faces a recognition and a warning; a most delicate recognition of what a foreigner had chanced to meet of misfortune on the fields of France; a most subtle warning that the day of the foreigner had nevertheless ended. Surely, surely something sharp, something fearful, something deeply resentful about Wilson and his policy was waiting to be spoken as soon as courtesy permitted. The moment the great door closed behind me it would issue, with sibilant clearness, from every pair of lips.

The echo of that unspoken word followed me in my drive past the captured guns piled on the place de la Concorde. Emblems of glorious victory? Sad, smoked milestones of a past already unreal and obscure? Spars washed ashore by the great wave of America's old love for France, France's old reliance on America? Beloved A.E.F., you had better hurry home. Dear Wilsonians, your footing on French soil grows precarious. In that electric-lighted Crillon, the focus of your earnest energies, the hive of your buzzing idealism, can you possibly detect what a Frenchman is saying and thinking behind an Henri IV door?

So it was for this division, this severing into rival camps and understandings, it was for these feuds born of our brains that our hearts brought us across the sea? The draft Covenant of the League of Nations is just to be presented. And I think of Spire's poem:

Et voila!
Il a fallu dix millions d'hommes,
Dix millions d'hommes couches a terre,
Sanglants, perces, ouverts;
Rdlant, sans une goutte d'eau pour leur fibvre,
Sans un baiser pour leurs levres.
Il a fallu dix millions d'hommes,
Pour ce vieux rive d'enfant,
Cette chose si simple.
Tu vas l'avoir, to Societe des Nations!
Chacun va livrer ses armes.
Chacun va livrer ses bateaux.
Plus de heurts, plus de chocs, plus de haines!

Plus de querelles, meme entre frbres!
Nous allons ouvrir un grand livre;
Nous allons peser Unties chores
Dans une surprecise balance:
Pour le juste, la recompense;
Pour le mechant, la peine juste;
Et le fils ne payera plus pour la faute du pbre.
Dix millions d'hommes, dix millions d'hommes
Que c'est peu, mon Dieu! que c'est peu
Pour tette chose si precieuse!

***

S.S. Rochambeau, May 10

WE steamed out of the port of le Havre at sunset. Several thousand doughboys crowded on the lower forward deck, clinging like great swarms of brown locusts to masts and spars, cheering in high falsetto, waving to the little weeping groups of French admirers on dock and jetty. But mostly facing, straining with an almost painful ecstacy to that lighted Western world hidden beyond the dip of the blue sea.

"Children, wonderful children," sighed Joe Smith from the rail beside me. "All soldiers are children. But ours are the youngest in history."

The soft veiled glow of the French May evening, falling wide across the water, seemed centred and concentrated on these youngest faces in history, giving them an epic look I can never forget. A look compounded of hunger for home and wistfulness at stern adventure ended; a look of new patience and old memory, and sharp, secret yearning for something bigger than earth and sea, and war and peace, which the sliding waves and the oncoming dark lifted almost into sublimity. How will the mothers and wives feel the first time they note that strange look in these faces... When, sitting apart in front of the little frame house, the man stares out, unseeing, beyond the prairie and the mountains.

The water swished and foamed, the air struck salt to our hearts, the grey roofs of France receded into the slaty night. But still a long streak of yellow flamed across our bow, and still a few black forms clung slant to the black spars, above the dim, crowded rows now stretched on the deck.

"I don't want to see no other port till I get to the Golden Gate. Best little old harbor in the world!"

"It is, *you* know!"

Will not the great unwritten American novel be the true story of two American buddies who came to France and went home again?

***

Lucinda has settled me in my steamer chair in the dark, and gone to walk off her blues with Joe. (A most sad Captain was left behind on the dock. The most deserted, most despairing Captain I have ever seen. I wish I dared to send him a wireless to-night, bidding him to lift up his spirit.) What a sense of liberation to have swung off into the fresh Atlantic currents away from illness and hospitals, away from Paris, where one seemed to be always

"Wandering between two worlds, one dead,

The other powerless to be born."

Ten days of detachment ahead, like the blessed detachment of the evacuation train.

Several months since I have tried to set down any impression of the outside world. It crowded too close, once I had ceased to see entirely with other people's eyes. My limping journeys into Paris disclosed a pattern too complex, a background too obscure. Americans growing always more depressed and baffled, Frenchmen more vindictive and dissatisfied, Italians more angry and headstrong, Englishmen more cocksure and domineering, and the protagonists of the smaller nations more futile and querulous. Wilson dwindling from a demi-god, justifying the fears of conservatives and deceiving the hopes of radicals. Ukraine and Hungary and Bavaria going Bolshevik, Bulgaria, Roumania, Poland, Czecho-Slovakia in ferment, Egypt, Korea in revolt. Spartacism spreading in Germany, Russia blockaded and starving, France startled by apparitions of bankruptcy and social revolution. The

Peace Conference muddling and floundering along in secrecy and doubt till it became the butt of every boulevard wit. Four days ago, on the anniversary of the sinking of the Lusitania, the compendium of its tragic labors was presented to the German delegates at Versailles.

***

And yet, how utterly inviolate the French countryside through which we journeyed this morning. It seemed that the giant fires which had burned the skies, and the jarring voices which had pierced the air but yesterday were quenched and stilled forever, and those velvet green undulations, those silver squares of beech-wood, those tufted grey villages preserved in some timeless ether to calm and exalt the souls of men. Will France be able to mellow her hazardous victory, as she mellows pears against those old red brick walls, and turn it into her ripe fruit of civilization?

It was characteristic of my excellent friend F. F. to turn up at that early morning boat train. His spirits were pristine like the hour, and he kept me jumping from one steep intellectual crag to another—to him a station platform is as good as any other for humane and political discourse and a lame leg no detriment to acrobatics—while Ernest and Joe and Lucinda engineered the vulgar bestowal of my luggage, and the finding of a seat. Gradually I became so heavily laden with problems of Zionism and of the universe, with books, and newspapers, and pressing messages for New York, Boston, and Connecticut, that I could scarcely climb aboard. We had begun to get up steam when he rushed back to call through the carriage window:

"Hoover told me yesterday he hasn't been able to get any food into Russia, in spite of the Allied promises. Tell the N.R. they *must* keep up the fight!"

Russia... In a private dining-room of a restaurant on the Champs Elysees we are six at the table. On the right of our cosmopolitan and accomplished hostess a face that is both mystical and material, lined and grey as fifty, yet in its plump contour decidedly less than forty. A round, shaven, pugilistic head. A pair of extraordinarily sensitive and beautiful hands which make staccato gestures. A voice that rises, harshly swells, suddenly drowns the tiny room in a flood of oratory big enough for the Trocadero. The mirrors and panelled doors seem to crack, but the voice roars on, condemning the Allies for lack of help in time of need, condemning the Bolsheviki, condemning Kolchak—till suddenly it breaks and shrivels on a note of truly Russian self-analysis and self-distrust:

"And they call me a weak man..."

At which our gifted Florentine host, in his diplomat's voice, hazards a smooth, underlined: *"Mais, M. le president..."*

The words are magic. Something like a bath of soothing oil spreads slowly over the cropped head and the grey face. Complacency dawns. The tense table draws a long breath and the tactful host inquires: "Now, M. Kerensky, what practical measures will you suggest to the Conference when you get a hearing?..."

But the voice only grumbles and thunders.

Then there was Bill Bullitt in his tweed suit, discoursing in an attic of the Crillon, immediately under that roof where an American sentry is even yet stalking gloomily up and down. (If he didn't, of course, spies might slip down the chimneys.) This heat, this vision, these definitive views for practical Allied action disturb the worthy statesmen in the ceremonial chambers below. He haunts them like a nightmare, but they won't allow him any daylight reality. Right or wrong, they have hidden their eyes and stopped their ears...

Just here appear Joe and Lucinda to break the thread of memory and guide my wobbly ankles over the slewing deck. Lucky person that I am to have two such charming, proven faces and four arms so steady to help me from the hospital to my family. For it was hard to leave Ernest behind.

"My God!" he suddenly broke out to F. F. on the platform. "She's going to see my wife in ten days.."

May 15

WHERE is that detachment of mine? I have left a hospital that had become a home, a garden where spring was stirring, for the maelstrom, the vortex, the processional of American democracy. All day past my chair they tramp, tramp, tramp. (Feet are miraculous to me now. I watch them as if they were mechanical toys.) Women war workers in their tailored clothes of many hues, demobilized ambulance men with orange ribbons, officers who have had their uniforms recut in France and learned to carry themselves easily. Portly spiritual advisers to the troops from central Illinois, whose insignia is a red triangle; bankers and lawyers from Oregon and Washington, marked with the red cross—in those skyscrapers to which they are returning they will, to the end of their days, be addressed as "major." Trig lieutenants late of some New York department store, guiding by an elbow girls from the East Fifties and Sixties who would once have resented it. Faces wracked, or grave, or flippant, buttonholes with decorations or without; those who have sealed their service in heart's blood, and those who have written it in sand and dust—round and round and round... Too pervasive, too pressing for an observer who has just emerged from a still, grey room.

Yet if I were Rodin or St. Gaudens, wanting to create for some spacious Washington vista a heroic monument to the American effort in France, I should ask no better than to be drawn into this monotonous procession. I should pause at the bow where a chaplain lifts up a flat voice to rows of blinking faces: "You are going back to an Era of Reconstruction... Bigger and Better America.." I should linger at the stern, where happier doughboys, perched on boats, console the piquant nostalgia of French war brides. And when evening came, and the decks grew silent and empty I should go out and commune with the swirl of the mid-Atlantic. And gradually these men and women and their varying purposes, their differences of temperament, and class, and organization would be fused and sublimated.

The monument that appeared out of the fog would differ from all other war monuments in one striking particular: behind the young soldier, following his bold, swinging movement across the sea with quieter rhythm, would come a feminine image—the American woman, first in history to follow her men to battle. I see her as a rather generalized athletic figure, of no special age, with a face worn to a serenity as immanent as that of a Greek grave relief. To pledge the souls of men against their destiny, however ugly and dark it appeared; to show the depth of human tenderness in an almost impersonal and universal spirit—this was what her service implied. This was what the soldiers themselves demanded of her, however far they wandered from Puritan pastures. Cheap flirtation, fine personal adventure, traditional romance... but beyond, behind, maintained at greater cost than the home-keeping women folk will ever know, the gallant comradeship of the sexes on which our civilization rests.

Somehow my synthesised American woman begins to looks very much like the vivid Gertrude, after all... Gertrude who appeared swiftly out of Germany in her blue coat on an April Sunday, to try to free some soldiers from prison. Up to the end my visitors continued to come thus, like messengers in Greek tragedy, bringing tidings from some far country.

The President was the supreme messenger of the gods, materializing out of a void with raised hand to speak words which should stay the course of Destiny. Little they seemed to avail. Yet, Wilson, Gertrude, F. F., are right in this: history is not something that happens but something to be fought for and directed by our own wills, something to be wrought out of the cross-purposes of Paris 1919 as well as out of the mud of the trenches. If Dr. M.'s knife had faltered by a fraction of an inch Mademoiselle V. would have died on the operating-table instead of smiling, as I left her, in the Neuilly garden.... If a new horse-chestnut leaf, blown by the tempest, falls here instead of there, the course of the world's progress will be changed... ah, there it goes, into the Seine, under the feet of a British statesman, crushed by the wheels of a sightseeing American truck which boasts that the debt to Lafayette is paid.

Poor President, we have asked him in his solitary person to be not merely the messenger of the gods, but the magician who would catch the leaf in mid-air, the sculptor who would mould the mud into marble, the surgeon who with one sure thrust would pierce the malady of Europe. Perhaps to speak words of divine humanity was his sole mission....

My ankles ache in the dark sea-damp. But I rest against the pulse of the engines throbbing, throbbing, throbbing like implacable time itself as we steam towards New York.

We all fear a little our encounter with that vast, tumultuous city, whose clangor comes to us dimly over the sea. What scorn of human destiny in that clangor, what fierceness of hope after a Europe of pain, and death, and despair....

We all dread a little the definition of the city's jagged outline. Famished, arrested faces of young wives begin to take shape on the dock. (How shall I greet one dear, wistful figure who somehow cannot help hoping he has come along..) Behind the wives, sisters, mothers, fathers—still faces listening for a tale that will never be told.

For adventure was only the keen edge of the experience with which our slow-moving Rochambeau is so heavy laden. Tragedy was its blade. I catch an arrowy flash in the clear American sunshine, where young men in civilian clothes move swift beyond the waiting crowds. Their busy patterns of new life are traced in something hard and bright.

Beyond the young men unscathed green country where children are at play. Quaint little face of Nancy, deliciously smiling under an Alice in Wonderland comb, in a garden that slopes down a hill. Scrambling of bare legs and arms, tinkling of lemonade in a white house on a Turnpike by a tidal river where a voice reads Froissart... History out of a book.

It is to-morrow which cows us, as a high tragedian said long ago. The Coming Thing, greater perhaps than to-day or yesterday, throbbing out its portent in the dark hospital night, looming and lurking behind the mirage of a familiar shore.

THE END

Made in the USA
Monee, IL
24 April 2021

66705163R00083